Olympic Laws

Olympic Laws: Culture, Values, Tensions is the first book to analyse fully the Olympic legal framework and its application to the IOC and the Olympic Games through a socio-legal lens. It opens up a new window into understanding the Olympic Games across recent iterations of the Games and on to future Games.

The book begins by defining the parameters of the emergent legal sub-fields of Sports Law, *lex Olympica* and Olympic Law, through the identification of the sources of these Olympic Laws and their underpinning norms. It then uses a series of case studies to demonstrate how lex Olympica has evolved as a means of defending the Olympic Movement from unwanted legal interventions, how Olympic Law has been created to protect the commercial rights vested in the Games, and how the legacies created by this unique category of law have a lasting impact on host cities and beyond. It concludes with a call that the IOC should recalibrate its relationships with prospective hosts and the participating athletes by requiring specific adherence to the Fundamental Principles of Olympism.

This is essential reading for any student or researcher with an interest in Olympic studies, sports law, or socio-legal studies or any practising lawyer or events professional looking to better understand the impact and institutions of mega-events.

Mark James is Professor of Sports Law at the Manchester Law School at Manchester Metropolitan University, UK.

Guy Osborn is Professor of Law at Westminster Law School, University of Westminster, UK.

Routledge Focus on Sport, Culture and Society

Routledge Focus on Sport, Culture and Society showcases the latest cutting-edge research in the sociology of sport and exercise. Concise in form (20,000-50,000 words) and published quickly (within three months), the books in this series represents an important channel through which authors can disseminate their research swiftly and make an impact on current debates. We welcome submissions on any topic within the socio-cultural study of sport and exercise, including but not limited to subjects such as gender, race, sexuality, disability, politics, the media, social theory, Olympic Studies, and the ethics and philosophy of sport. The series aims to be theoretically-informed, empirically-grounded and international in reach, and will include a diversity of methodological approaches.

Available in this series:

On Boxing
Critical Interventions in the Bittersweet Science
Joseph D Lewandowski

Sport, Forced Migration and the 'Refugee Crisis'
Enrico Michelini

Sport Policy Across the United Kingdom
A Comparative Analysis
Edited by Mathew Dowling, Spencer Harris and Chris Mackintosh

Olympic Laws
Culture, Values, Tensions
Mark James and Guy Osborn

For more information about this series, please visit: https://www.routledge.com/Routledge-Focus-on-Sport-Culture-and-Society/book-series/RFSCS

Olympic Laws
Culture, Values, Tensions

Mark James and Guy Osborn

Routledge
Taylor & Francis Group

LONDON AND NEW YORK

First published 2024
by Routledge
4 Park Square, Milton Park, Abingdon, Oxon OX14 4RN

and by Routledge
605 Third Avenue, New York, NY 10158

Routledge is an imprint of the Taylor & Francis Group, an informa business

© 2024 Mark James and Guy Osborn

British Library Cataloguing-in-Publication Data
A catalogue record for this book is available from the British Library

ISBN: 978-0-367-33993-7 (hbk)
ISBN: 978-1-032-56254-4 (pbk)
ISBN: 978-0-429-32335-5 (ebk)

DOI: 10.4324/9780429323355

Typeset in Times New Roman
by KnowledgeWorks Global Ltd.

Contents

Acknowledgements

This book is the culmination of ideas that we have been working on for many years. During that time, we have had the advice and support of many people and are grateful to them all for the time that they have given freely to us. For both of us, much of our inspiration for working in this area comes from two people: Steve Redhead and Ken Foster. Their insight into and theoretical perspectives on sports law as it emerged as a new field of study have shaped much of our thinking on lex Olympica and Olympic law, and we are grateful for their ongoing presence in our work.

1 The Olympics: Culture, Values, Tensions

Introduction

This book represents the culmination of over a decade of research and writing on law and the Olympics. Using the emerging field of *lex Olympica* and Olympic law as a critical lens, our aim is to explore the tension between the International Olympic Committee's (IOC's) stated culture the values embodied in Olympism and the commercialisation of the Olympic Games. Focussing on the legality of the restrictive impact of the Olympic legal framework on athletes, we argue that this clash between culture and commerce within the Olympic Movement is unbalanced and that a recalibration of the relationship is needed to achieve a workable equilibrium.

We first flagged this tension, this idea of a problematic cultural-commercial interface, in an article for the *Modern Law Review* in 2011,[1] and much of the research into discrete areas of the Olympic legal framework that we have pursued in the intervening years has had the consideration of this tension at its core. The idea behind writing this book was to draw out these issues and make this tension explicit. Further to this, our aim is to propose how the tensions identified throughout can be ameliorated by taking a more relational approach to interpreting the contracts between the IOC and its key stakeholders. Between signing the contract for the book and its delivery, the Covid-19 pandemic intervened. This had a number of impacts, including that, to a degree, it forced the Olympic Movement itself to consider specifically its aims, ethos, and scope. It has, without question, accelerated consideration of, and intensified the need for, a radical rethinking of the Olympic Games and its underpinning ideals after two editions, Tokyo 2020 and Beijing 2022, took place during the pandemic. Although both of these events provide useful ways to explore the key tensions that are central to the book, our focus is primarily on Tokyo 2020 as many of the issues relating to athletes' rights, including in particular the impact on them of Rules 40 and 50 of the Olympic Charter, came to a head in the months preceding and during this edition of the Games.

DOI: 10.4324/9780429323355-1

The Olympics divides. Tokyo 2020 was no exception. Writing *before* the global pandemic, Boykoff and Gaffney noted that whilst the IOC rhetoric for Tokyo 2020 was of 'recovery and reconstruction' following the 2011 tsunami and earthquake and the avowedly manifest benefits to Japanese society of hosting the Games, a counter-narrative was emerging. This included a week-long anti-Olympic summit of public lectures, workshops, field trips, and more: '[sports] mega-events like the Olympics have become flashpoints for anti-capitalist struggle, with the Games' negative social and ecological repercussions becoming increasingly evident.'[2] The pandemic accentuated and ossified this division. In May 2021, a month before Tokyo 2020 was due to begin, a Nikkei/Tokyo TV survey found substantial opposition to the event taking place, with 62% of the sample responding that the Games should be cancelled or postponed, and just 1% replying that they should go ahead with a full audience.[3] This was for an event that had *already* been postponed from 2020 to 2021, although maintaining its original title because of its economic importance. Ironically, for a body like the IOC that zealously guards the intellectual property of the Olympic iconography, if the Games had proved to be a super-spreader event, the IOC would have looked less approvingly upon their own Covid strain, the Tokyo 2020® variant, had that come to pass.[4]

Whilst there was specific opposition to the staging of Tokyo 2020, general opposition to the Olympics is not purely a modern construct:

[movements] around the world have expressed their concerns and opposition to the Olympics and Olympism, and recorded the "side effects" of the world's biggest sporting event: the dubious use of public money, gentrification, harassment, threats to the environmental and social balance and other controversies that have affected the hosting and bidding cities.[5]

As sites where power is frequently exercised by states and other international actors, where significant degrees of international cooperation are on display, and where political symbolism is routinely evoked, the Olympics are ripe for scholarly analysis.[6] Recent Games have been subject to intense, and often fierce, criticism at both local and international levels.[7] Some of these narratives and counter-narratives are dealt with below and returned to later in the book. First, however, we explore some of the specificities of Tokyo 2020 and articulate and explain the extraordinary reach and power of the IOC.

Tokyo 2020 as a watershed moment

Before the Games began, doubts were cast on the safety of Tokyo 2020, and the specific and myriad ethical and health challenges posed by it, taking place in mid-summer and during a pandemic.[8] Outside of any broader protests, the 'problem' of Tokyo 2020 and whether the Games could, or should, be cancelled was laid bare by McCurry:

> Only the IOC has the authority to cancel the Games. But if Japan decided to turn them into a practical impossibility by, for example, imposing watertight travel restrictions on all overseas visitors, it would have to bear the costs and compensate the IOC for any losses resulting from claims by third parties.[9]

Anderson amplified this, noting the extraordinariness of the IOC in general, and of Tokyo 2020 specifically.[10] It is indeed extraordinary that a private entity can exercise such influence over public authorities. Further, the Host City Contract (HCC), now known as the Olympic Host Contract, is an extraordinary document in itself in terms of the requirements that it imposes on both the host state and the local organising committee. Referencing Tokyo 2020, Anderson highlighted two particularly problematic clauses. First, clause 72, the impact of which was that:

> If, over the next few weeks [prior to the Opening Ceremony], the Japanese government seeks to pass a law or even a public health regulation, which has adverse consequences for the hosting of the Games (and thus adverse commercial consequences for the IOC), this could be considered a breach of contract. And this would justify termination of the contract by the IOC.

Secondly, clause 66, which contains the full range of powers invested in the IOC to unilaterally terminate the HCC. This incredibly wide-ranging clause effectively permits the IOC to walk away from the contract without consequence, but allows for no such reciprocal power for the hosts.

The question whether Tokyo 2020 can be seen as a success is not a straightforward one.[11] Given the divisions identified throughout this chapter, the answer will differ depending on who is asked, and the lens through which their answers are examined. For athletes, it was a qualified success, notwithstanding the lack of crowds and the reduced Olympic experience. Many athletes expressed joy that they had even made it to Tokyo 2020 after five long and often difficult years. At a local level, of Japan's 58 medals, well over half were won by women, representing a significant achievement for a somewhat traditional and patriarchal society. Cases of Covid-19 spiked, however, and the final cost was put conservatively at $15.4 billion. The IOC was not obliged under the HCC to contribute anything to the ballooning costs, whilst, at the same time, cementing their own financial security through generous and long-term broadcasting deals. In terms of *consuming* the Games, Majumdar noted that although of all the Olympics he had attended this was the hardest to cover, and the most tortuous to prepare for, it was also the most 'different' in a more positive sense, as it demonstrated how the Games can operate in such a changed environment:

> [what] Tokyo has also taught us is that mega spectacles can be organised with proper protocols in place … In Paris, expected to be staged in a covid-contained world, we will see a hybrid model emerge – take the best of the past and merge it with the learnings from the new normal. In that sense Tokyo will forever remain a watershed.[12]

Looking at a more negative aspect of its impact, Duigan and Mair stress the divisions created by hosting the Olympics.[13] They examine specifically the legacies claimed for Tokyo 2020, and how the positive pre-Games rhetoric has not been borne out by post-Games reality, with rising property prices and rents, and increased corporate colonisation amongst the negative and divisive upshots. A further negative legacy is that much of the anti-Tokyo 2020 sentiment is being channelled into protests against the bid to host the Sapporo 2030 Winter Games.[14]

Whilst Tokyo 2020 is an interesting case study in and of itself, the key to any understanding of the Olympics is to appreciate its cyclical nature; no sooner has one edition ended than another appears on the mega event horizon. The legacy period of one Games is the pregnancy period of another, and later chapters discuss how these events learn from, and respond to, the experiences of their predecessors. This cyclical nature was even more pronounced with the Beijing 2022 Winter Games taking place less than seven months after the Tokyo 2020 closing ceremony.

The divisions, the differences of opinion, and the arguments for and against the Olympic Games are also repeated in a cyclical fashion. Not only does the Olympics divide, but at its heart is a series of dialectics. Segrave has stated that '[a]s in ancient times, Olympism is the manifestation of a fundamental dialectic between body and soul, existence and essence, individual and group, and competition and cooperation.'[15] Chatziefstathiou notes an inherent contradiction within Olympism, particularly around our understanding of Olympic philosophy and how it is contested.[16] These tensions include those between the natural environment and the organisation of the Games,[17] between 'gift' Olympism and 'commodity' Olympism,[18] and, more fundamentally, the ideals of Olympism and the commercial reality of the Olympics in practice.[19]

A relatively recent and pertinent example of this tension was seen, very publicly, in the controversy that erupted at Sochi 2014 concerning Russia's so-called 'anti-gay laws' and their apparent conflict with the Fundamental Principles of Olympism. Prior to the Games, protestors across 19 cities gathered for a 'global speak out' and activists called for a boycott of Sochi 2014.[20] Whilst some protestors cited Principle 4 with its focus on sport as a human right as their impetus, others, us included, focussed on the applicability of Principle 6, which stated that:

> The enjoyment of the rights and freedoms set forth in this Olympic Charter shall be secured without discrimination of any kind, such as race, colour, sex, language, religion, political or other opinion, national or social origin, property, birth or other status.

The Russian legislation in force at the time allowed the state to fine, and potentially detain, individuals who promoted material relating to non-traditional sexual relations to minors.[21] This has been interpreted as meaning that the promotion of homosexuality and homosexual relationships is a criminal offence. In contrast, Principle 6 requires signatories to uphold the Olympic Charter without discrimination *of any kind*. To add to the complexity of the situation, Rule 50(2) of the Olympic Charter prohibits any demonstration or distribution of political, religious, or racial propaganda at Olympic sites, venues, or other controlled areas.[22] This resulted in three linked, but often misunderstood, Olympic legal outcomes. First, the clearly discriminatory Russian legislation was in breach of the covenant provided by the Russian state that it would guarantee respect for the Olympic Charter, as required by Rule 33 of the Olympic Charter and evidenced in the Sochi 2014 bid documentation.[23] Secondly, the IOC could take no action against either of the key Russian signatories of the HCC, the Russian Olympic Committee and the Sochi Organising Committee, as neither was in breach of the Charter as these two bodies were not acting in a discriminatory manner. Thirdly, athletes were prohibited from protesting against the Russian law as to do so would risk disqualification by breaching Rule 50(2) and Russian law; they were, however, free to promote the anti-discrimination message of Principle 6.[24]

Looking more broadly at the valorisation of the Olympics Games and the wider Olympic Movement, Henry presents six dimensions of costs and benefits: the cultural, economic, political, social, environmental, and sporting.[25] We would argue further that the Olympics can be presented as a series of positive and negative binaries and also that the Olympic legal framework should be added as a seventh dimension. We maintain that the essence of this dialectic is a tension between the *commercial* and the *cultural*, which this book seeks to illustrate by examining how these opposing forces have manifested themselves through a legal lens. We begin with a consideration of what Olympic culture is and introduce the key Olympic principles that underpin the Olympic Movement.

Olympic principles and Olympic culture

Throughout its history, the IOC has developed a series of guiding principles that are supposed to underpin the rationale for the existence of the Olympic Movement and the celebration of the Olympic Games.[26] The Fundamental

Principles of Olympism provide a corporate mission statement at the start of the Olympic Charter and should be read alongside the IOC's recommendations for the development of the Olympic Movement in their Agenda 2020+5 document,[27] its commitment to sustainability,[28] and the implementation of Strategic Framework on Human Rights.[29] Pound makes the point that until the 1980s, the term 'Olympic values' was primarily a philosophical construct,[30] but with the arrival of a new IOC President and the Los Angeles 1984 Games, the tension between the Olympic values and economic interests became increasingly prominent.[31] As the Olympic Movement undergoes increasing academic and political scrutiny, alongside the increasing sophistication of the NOlympics movement, the tensions between what the IOC claims that it stands for and what it actually does stand for are brought into stark contrast. These tensions were accelerated by the IOC requiring the Tokyo 2020 edition of the Olympics to go ahead during a global pandemic, whilst a state of emergency was in place in Tokyo and other host cities, and the human rights and environmental concerns of hosting the 2022 Winter Games in Beijing, China.

These latest editions of the Olympics have called into question the IOC's real priorities much more publicly than has previously been the case. Issues concerning the financing of the Games and the debt incurred by host cities,[32] the imbalance of the HCC, equality and discrimination,[33] the environmental impact of hosting the Olympics,[34] and their overall impact on hosting communities have been the focus of wide-ranging critical analyses by advocacy groups and academics.[35] Amongst the most high-profile of these issues are the regulation of the competing athletes by the Olympic Charter and the participation agreements that they have to sign to secure accreditation to appear in the Games. These are the respective foci of the analyses in Chapters 3 and 4.

The philosophy of Olympism has underpinned the evolution of the modern Olympic Movement since its inception, though the process of its codification began only as recently as the 1991 version of the Olympic Charter. Since then, it has evolved into what are now defined as the Fundamental Principles of Olympism, the importance of which can be seen by their placement at the start of the Olympic Charter and their influence on the meaning and justification of the Rules that follow. The modern editions of the Games are underpinned by these seven core Olympic principles, including stressing the educational value of sport, and the importance of blending culture with education. Rule 2 of the Olympic Charter states that the mission of the IOC is to promote Olympism throughout the world and to lead the Olympic Movement. Subsections 1–16 of Rule 2 provide additional detail, explaining that the IOC's role includes (but is not limited to): encouraging and supporting the promotion of ethics and good governance in sport; the education of youth through sport; ensuring that the spirit of fair play prevails and violence is banned; ensuring the regular celebration of the Olympic Games; endeavouring to place sport at the service of humanity and thereby to promote peace; preserving the autonomy of sport;

acting against any form of discrimination affecting the Olympic Movement; encouraging the promotion of women in sport at all levels; promoting the principle of equality of men and women; protecting clean athletes and the integrity of sport; opposing any political or commercial abuse of sport and its athletes; encouraging a responsible concern for environmental issues; promoting sustainable development in sport; and encouraging initiatives blending sport with culture and education.

It is clear from this exposition of the finer points of the IOC's mission that its avowed focus is on promoting the underpinning spirit of sport, on sport being a driver of education, health, and peace, and viewing sport as an element of culture. The only mention of the commercial exploitation of sport is in Rule 2(10), where the IOC's mission is 'to *oppose* any ... commercial abuse of sport and athletes' (our emphasis). This focus on promoting sport alongside education and culture is reinforced by the inclusion of the Fundamental Principles of Olympism at the start of the Olympic Charter, before the Rules are enunciated, as a corporate mission statement and interpretative matrix. This extended definition of Olympism has developed into seven guiding Principles. At one extreme, these include manifesto-style statements that Olympism is a philosophy of life, the goal of which is to promote a peaceful society and preserve human dignity, and that the practice of sport is a human right.[36] At the other are Principle 5, which promotes the autonomy of sports governance from political interference, and Principle 6,[37] which prohibits amongst all signatories of the Charter discrimination of any kind, and in particular where it is grounded in race, colour, sex, sexual orientation, language, religion, political or other opinion, national or social origin, property, and birth or other status. Finally, Principle 7 requires that all members of the Olympic Movement are signatories of, and act in compliance with, the Olympic Charter. This ensures that the majority of the main international sports federations, including their constituent associations, clubs, athletes, and officials, all National Olympic Committees (NOCs), and any extant organising committees of forthcoming editions of the Olympic Games are bound by the Rules of the Olympic Charter.[38] What is less clear is the extent to which the host state, which is not a signatory of the Olympic Charter, is bound by its requirements. Rule 33 requires a legally binding guarantee that the host government and public authorities will act in compliance with the Olympic Charter. A failure to comply with the terms of the covenant, which is submitted as part of the Candidate City File, is a breach of the HCC, which, at least technically, could result in the removal of the invitation to host the Games. It can, therefore, be argued that even host governments are bound by the values inherent in Olympism, though this has never been explored as a means of securing changes to national laws of the host legal system.

This unequivocal statement of what it is that the Olympic Movement in general, and the IOC in particular, represents is at odds not only with other parts of the Charter itself but also with the way that the IOC and the various organising committees conduct their commercial business, something we noted at the outset of the book. As Toohey and Veal have observed:

> The "spirit" of Olympism is ostensibly non-materialist: the alliance between Olympism and commerce is therefore potentially a fragile one … Olympism enshrines certain ideals which, as with a religion, its custodians are sworn to uphold. Many see commercialisation as undermining these ideals.[39]

Rule 7 of the Olympic Charter exerts the IOC's ownership of the Olympic Games and the Olympic Properties, listed in Rules 8–14 as the Olympic symbol, flag, motto, emblems, anthem, flame, torch, and designations (where the Olympic Rings are incorporated into the logo of a separate entity, such as a NOC). The importance of the Olympic Properties to the Olympic Movement can be summarised succinctly:

> The meaning and the values of Olympism are conveyed by symbols. Among these are the rings, the motto and the flame. These symbols transmit a message in a simple and direct manner. They give the Games and the Olympic Movement an identity.[40]

Beyond culture: The role of commerce

This cultural and iconic value has, however, been overshadowed by the immense commercial value of the intellectual property associated with the Olympic Games. The commercial and intellectual property rights are variously protected by the Nairobi Treaty on the Protection of the Olympic Symbol 1981,[41] registrations of the Rings and other properties as international trademarks, and specific national legislation that vests the right to the commercial exploitation of the Properties in either the home NOC, an organising committee of an upcoming edition of the Olympics, or the IOC. The Nairobi Treaty is administered by the World Intellectual Property Organisation and requires signatories to refuse to register, or to invalidate the registration of the Olympic Symbol (the Rings) as a trademark, and to prohibit the use for commercial purposes of any sign consisting of or containing the Rings, except with the IOC's authorisation or under an appropriate licence. There are currently 54 signatories to the Nairobi Treaty, including only Brazil and Russia as recent or prospective host countries. Further protection can be provided by jurisdiction-specific national legislation. For example, from a British perspective, the Olympic Symbol (Protection) Act 1995 restricts the use of the Olympic Rings, the words Olympic, Olympian, and Olympiad (and their plural and Paralympic equivalents), and Olympic motto except by, or with the permission of, the British Olympic Association and the British Paralympic Association.[42] In the United States of America, the Amateur Sports Act of

1978, later amended in 1998 by the Ted Stevens Olympic and Amateur Sports Act, grants similar exclusive domestic commercial rights to the United States Olympic and Paralympic Committee.

Not only does the IOC require these legislative protections for the benefit of its commercial partners and those of each edition of the Olympic Games, but it is also extremely proactive in protecting its brand. The result is that the legal norms created and developed by the IOC for itself, the Olympic Games, and their commercial partners require the implementation of specific laws in the host nation. In contradistinction, Olympism is found only in the preamble to the Charter and is not required to be promoted or protected by the host legislature. Instead, it is merely expected that the organising committee, as a signatory of the Charter, will take appropriate steps to promote the philosophy of the Olympic Movement as an integral part of its hosting of the Games. This disjunction is crucial and forms the bedrock of the tension between the Olympic values and the commercialisation of the Games. It is the examination of this tension that, we argue, gives rise to the need to recalibrate the relationship between the Olympic Movement and its key stakeholders and, in particular, the athletes.

The Charter also references that sport is a human right (Principle 4) and that 'The goal of Olympism is to place sport at the service of the harmonious development of humankind, with a view to promoting a peaceful society concerned with the preservation of human dignity' (Principle 2). Further, the modern Olympics were born out of a desire to link sport and education, although even this was built on myth and distortion, based as it is on a 19th century British vision of sport having a formative role within educational development, forged largely from British public school understandings of these concepts. The early modern Games were, in many ways, elitist, sexist, and racist, with little adherence to the Olympic ethos and spirit.[43] These values and aspirations are laudable, but it is questionable whether they ever matched the reality.

More recent critiques of the Olympic Games and the Olympic Movement have focussed less on the ethical and cultural, and spoken more of disillusion, disenfranchisement, and corruption.[44] That said, the rhetoric of the Olympic Charter and its underpinning justification was that sport fulfilled an important social function that could be an important catalyst for change. These conceptions appear to be hard to reconcile with '[a] global conglomerate [that] generates enormous profits, consumes entire television networks for weeks at a time, and has spawned a *lingua franca* that simultaneously reinforces and transcends national and cultural borders.'[45] This issue of globalisation and commercialisation is crucial. The Olympics as a concept or project cannot be considered without understanding its role as a global entertainment force. Indeed, the globalisation of the Games has given rise to some of the tensions that the Olympic Movement has had to confront, '[because] the Olympics are a truly global phenomenon – in many ways a uniquely global event – they manifest all of the ethical issues and dilemmas which have accompanied the process of globalisation in recent years.'[46]

Whilst the sporting aspect is obviously key, mega events such as the Olympics go beyond sport and have economic, social, and cultural consequences. To Hayes and Karamichas' list could be added the environmental, political, and legal dimensions of hosting the Games.[47] Writing about London 2012, we analysed whether the tension between the increasing economic and commercial significance of the Games can be reconciled with the spirit of Olympism. Responding later to the Olympic Agenda 2020, we noted that:

> [during] our research, a recurrent theme has emerged concerning the inter-relationship between the educational and philosophical ethos of Olympism, and the broader commercial imperatives of the modern-day Olympic Movement, and particularly in terms of staging an edition of the Games. This recurrent theme has identified and detailed a tension between these two poles, and a debate as to whether the balance has been correctly drawn, and whether this is in need of recalibration.[48]

We return to recalibration in the final chapter, with examples and arguments explored in the intervening chapters, but first some broad commercial counterpoints to the Olympic ethos and philosophy must be outlined. Smart notes that commercialism has gathered momentum throughout the modern Olympic era and that even in 1896 there were emergent signs of this tension, whilst Los Angeles 1984 provided the paradigm shift, or as Tomlinson argued, 'the mobilization of private capital, integral to the LA Games, dramatically reframed the Olympic project as a commercial product and prime commodity for the global media.'[49]

This shift in momentum and focus towards a commercial frame is evidenced in a variety of ways. Smart explores this through examining consumer merchandising revenue from licenses.[50] This shows a significant increase in revenue through the 1992 to 2012 period; at Barcelona 1992, revenue from this source was $17.2m, increasing to $119m by London 2012. It is also lucrative to be linked to these mega sporting events through exclusive sponsorship arrangements, and this allure has encouraged the adoption of what might be termed creative associative behaviour. Ambush marketing, as this is often termed, is an amorphous concept.[51] In essence, it embraces situations where non-sponsors attempt to derive financial, and perhaps cultural, capital by associating themselves with an event without paying the fees required of official sponsors and partners. Writing about Sochi 2014, we noted that:

> Sporting mega-events of this nature attract ambush marketing campaigns almost as a matter of course, with advertisers trying either to piggyback on the worldwide media interest surrounding the event or to deliberately and specifically undermine the exclusive arrangements entered into by the primary rights holders and an official sponsor that is a corporate rival of the ambusher.[52]

The efforts put in place by the IOC in an attempt to combat and usurp these forms of behaviour are remarkable; all the more so when juxtaposed with their responses to regulate and enforce Olympism more generally. This exemplifies the tensions between culture and commerce, and the critical importance to the IOC of protecting its income streams over its commitment to the broader ideals of Olympism. Smart argues that commercial imperatives have compromised the Olympic ideals with the effect of consumerism undermining the ethos and function of sport itself.[53] All of these discussions force us to consider the purpose of the Games.

What are the Olympics for?

For Hayes and Karamichas, the legitimising discourse for events was usually based on claims of social transformation and legacy.[54] The periods of pregnancy, delivery, and legacy of an Olympic Games tend to see positive rhetoric presented. For example, Sebastian Coe, Chair of the London Organising Committee of the Olympic Games, outlined a four-pronged justification for hosting the Olympics as part of the bid to host the 2012 edition. This included an unforgettable experience for the athletes themselves, the forging of a British sporting legacy, the regeneration of East London, and of acting as a champion for the Olympic Movement more generally. The success of these aspirations is not easy to assess. Whilst many athletes might argue that the Games were a great success, and there were many unforgettable moments that have entered the sporting vernacular and become imprinted on the collective memory, in terms of sporting legacy, it is more difficult to evidence, let alone to valorise, its impact. East London has certainly changed beyond recognition, but much of this may have happened without the Olympic effect, given the ongoing eastward shift of the UK capital's centre of gravity. Others have seen less visible, and less desirable, legacies that were not considered when pitching to host the Games. Boykoff and Fussey explain that 'the 2012 London Olympics engendered legacies not touted in bid materials: a revamped security state, securitised neighbourhoods and riled up activist communities.'[55] These, they argue, are shadow legacies as they do not form part of the official narrative.

Smith goes further and has argued that whilst sports mega events such as the Olympics are often used as social and economic development tools, critics see these as an ineffective substitute for strategic urban policy and that such justifications are often little more than an excuse for expensive vanity projects.[56] This compounds the tension between the Olympic Movement's values and the IOC's exploitation of the brand. Do we need new stadiums instead of upgrading existing facilities and providing improved community sporting infrastructures? A new Olympic Village instead of increases in social housing provision? New venues built on protected environments?

Whilst a positive legacy is one (usually the official) narrative, there is, at the same time, a substantial counter-narrative, exemplified by the work of Boykoff[57] and Lenskyj,[58] who make strong arguments against the Games from a variety of perspectives. These counter-narratives provide ample evidence of the contested views of the Olympics and the tensions examined here. To return to one of our central themes, Smart notes the incompatibility of the two poles of commerce and culture:

> While the formative ideals of the Olympic Movement have endured, and to a degree continue to decorate the structure and organisation of the IOC, they are increasingly incompatible with the financial imperatives, commercial ethos and culture of consumption integral to the Olympic Games.[59]

Even the IOC is cognisant of these potential problems, with a consultation resulting in a number of recommendations in Agenda 2020,[60] and ultimately Agenda 2020+5. A moot point is whether Agenda 2020 has actually achieved anything of substance. Writing in 2014, Duval argued with prescience that any fundamental change on the back of Agenda 2020 was unlikely, but that for real change to be fomented, 'public scrutiny and societal irritation' were key.[61]

The impact of this public push for change was seen with the Principle 6 protests at Sochi 2014, where the relevance of the Olympic Charter, in terms of its enforceability and applicability, was telling. The controversy centred on Russia's 'anti-gay' laws and led directly to a proposal, unanimously accepted by the IOC as part of the Agenda 2020 reforms, to extend the protections afforded by Principle 6 to include specifically sexual orientation. It is generally assumed that the provisions of the Olympic Charter are only enforceable against its signatories; the signatories are contracting parties and the Charter forms an integral part of the interlocking series of contracts that form the cornerstone of *lex sportiva* in general and *lex Olympica* in particular.[62] However, the covenants provided by host governments as required by Rule 33 of the Olympic Charter indicate that compliance is also expected of the host state. Thus, where the Russian law provided the impetus for the amendment to Principle 6, the Olympic Charter could concomitantly have been used as a means to facilitate a change in Russian law. Although this level of political interference in a host's laws has hitherto only been considered appropriate to protect Olympic revenue streams, it does at least provide the IOC with the scope to act more politically, should it wish to do so. This could include requiring the host state to implement legal changes that provide benefits to the general populace whilst ensuring that it is discharging its responsibilities under the Charter.

Although such a move would be controversial, it would only echo the IOC's demands in other areas. The IOC exhibits no reservations about insisting on the implementation of legislative protections for its commercial properties and other 'perks' that assist in the smooth running of the Games.[63] There is, therefore, no obvious reason why it could not insist on legislative amendments that promote and protect the philosophy of Olympism, in particular its principles of non-discrimination, sustainability and environmentalism,[64] and human rights. This could take the form of specific legislation or a requirement that the host nation is a signatory of specific international conventions, treaties, and charters.[65] Although such an extension of the IOC's indirect law-making capabilities would be controversial, there would be nothing to prevent the IOC from requiring host legislatures to provide guarantees on basic human rights protections and compliance with minimum standards of protection for workers' rights, particularly those engaged on Olympic infrastructure projects, just as nothing has stopped it from requiring commercial protections and tax exemptions in the form of national laws.

For much of the recent past, the IOC has had such high levels of leverage over candidate cities that it could, and arguably should, have used this position to recalibrate its relationships and impose its own legal norms on actual and prospective hosts. Instead, the focus of its indirect legislative capability has been on the more effective and efficient exploitation of its commercial rights. The IOC's approval and implementation of the Strategic Framework on Human Rights still does not require host states to be compliant with specific relevant international treaties.[66] It reinforces that the parties to the HCC must be compliant with the Charter and applicable treaties; however, these protections can be seen as something of a hollow victory as the requirement is only that there is compliance with the international agreements, laws, and regulations already applicable in the host country. Thus, not only is there no requirement that the host country legislate to improve social, cultural, employment, environmental, and human rights protections, those bound by the HCC need only comply with the rights frameworks of the host, not those of the wider international community. Promotion and protection of social, cultural, environmental, and human rights requirements and guarantees would be much more in keeping with the underpinning ethos of Olympism, though whether such forced law creation could be actualised is a moot point.[67] It would, however, provide an effective counterbalance to the commercialisation of the Olympic philosophy.

Conclusion

The IOC, the Olympic Movement, and the Olympic Games themselves are undergoing unparalleled levels of critical scrutiny from activists, professional organisations, and academics across an array of causes and disciplines. The Olympics are no longer accepted by an unquestioning majority as a force for good, with even the IOC beginning, tentatively, to address some of these issues through its Agenda 2020 reform programme. However, the future viability of the Olympics is by no means certain.

This book engages with these debates from a legal perspective, critically examining how the law can be used by key stakeholders, particularly athletes, to challenge the Olympic normative framework through legal action. It examines two key contentions surrounding the creation and application of Olympic legal norms: that the ability of the IOC to impose its will through the creation of law needs to be recalibrated and its use monitored more explicitly; and that the balance between the ongoing commercialisation of the Olympic Games and the core educational and cultural ethos embedded in the Fundamental Principles of Olympism needs to be recalibrated. This is an important intervention as it develops and builds upon existing theories and concepts relating to transnational organisations, but applies these in a novel and singular context, providing support for a more balanced and arguably relational approach, to be adopted within the Olympic legal framework.

The rescheduled Tokyo 2020 Games are used as the focal point of these analyses, as it is likely to be seen in the future as a decisive moment in the history of the Olympic Movement. The implementation of various NOCs' guidance of what, to them, would be acceptable advertising under Rule 40 at Tokyo 2020 resulted in its successful challenge before the German competition authorities and led to a complete reframing of the IOC's approach to athlete advertising.[68] Similarly, the publication of the IOC's first guidance on the application of Rule 50 in January 2020, against the global backdrop of the Black Lives Matter protests, created the parameters within which athlete protests were considered acceptable to the IOC.[69] Together with the enforcement of the Host City Contract by the IOC to ensure that the 2020 Games took place during a global pandemic, these issues highlight the importance of legal analyses in debates about the future of the Olympics:

> The real future challenge for the IOC is to ensure the underlying values of sport, indeed the basic integrity of sport, are maintained, promoted and enforced. Those values are the necessary constant theme, the axis around which sport must rotate and without which sport cannot exist … it is actions that will be needed regarding the values of sport, not the mere recitation of those values.[70]

This chapter has explored the tensions at the heart of the Olympics. Starting from the premise that the 'Olympics divides,' and using Tokyo 2020 as its point of departure, it explored a series of dialectics, showing how each can be seen from a legal perspective. At the heart of this chapter has been an attempt to unpick the tension between commerce and culture; this tension is then reinforced, and amplified through specific treatment in the following chapters. Chapter 2 examines the role of the IOC and its unique ability, as a non-state actor, to create 'Olympic law' from its own internal norms, the *lex Olympica*. This new law operates for the benefit of the IOC itself, the wider Olympic Movement and, in particular, their sponsors and commercial partners. This creates an inherent tension between the promotion of Olympic culture and the protection of Olympic commercial rights, developing the idea we introduced in this chapter; that the IOC chooses to use legal mechanisms to protect its income, but not the Fundamental Principles of Olympism. Chapter 3 explores the tension between the right of athletes to earn a living through sport and Olympic commercial protectionism by examining the justiciability of *lex Olympica* following the successful challenge before the German competition authorities to the restrictions imposed by Rule 40 of the Olympic Charter, which imposes restrictions on athletes' ability to advertise during the Olympic Games. Here, the income of the IOC is prioritised at the expense of the earning potential of athletes, adding a further layer of tension to the relationship. Chapter 4 examines the legality of the restrictions imposed on athletes' ability to engage in protest and activism at the Olympics and the ways that this has evolved under the threat of legal challenge as an unlawful restriction on freedom of expression, highlighting the tension between the IOC's commitment to protecting and respecting human rights and its restriction of them by Rule 50. This shows a tension between the human rights rhetoric the IOC espouses and the restrictions it places on athletes' own human rights. In both Chapter 3 and Chapter 4, the tension between *lex Olympica* and the law is examined and contrasted with the Olympic law that the IOC requires to be created by a host.

The book concludes by arguing for a radical reappraisal of the IOC's lawmaking capabilities and their relationship with the Fundamental Principles of Olympism. This is examined through a critical analysis of the effects and implications of this law creation process more generally and develops from relational contract theory a more cooperative and accountable approach that potentially removes the impact of the tensions identified.[71] This includes the possibility of re-evaluating the Olympic Charter to reflect the broader Olympic community and embedding human rights and the rule of law in the Olympic legal framework, one of the stated aims of the Strategic Framework. To explore this, we must first turn to examine the role of the IOC within the Olympic legal framework.

Notes

1 James M and Osborn G (2011) 'London 2012 and the Impact of the UK's Olympic and Paralympic Legislation: Protecting Commerce or Preserving Culture?' 74(3) *Modern Law Review* 410–429.
2 Boykoff, J and Gaffney, C (2020) 'The Tokyo 2020 Games and the End of Olympic History' 31(2) *Capitalism, Nature, Socialism* 1–19, at 1.

3 Nikkei Asia (2021) 'Suga's approval rating plumbs new depths as emergency drags on' *Nikkei Asia*, 31 May, available at: https://asia.nikkei.com/Politics/Suga-s-approval-rating-plumbs-new-depths-as-emergency-drags-on (last accessed 27/01/2022).

4 Lies, E and Swift, R (2021) 'Tokyo Games could lead to Olympic coronavirus variant - Japanese doctor' *Reuters*, 27 May, available at: https://www.reuters.com/lifestyle/sports/japan-reassures-olympics-can-be-safe-extended-state-emergency-eyed-2021-05-27/ (last accessed 27/01/2022).

5 Zervas, K (2012) 'Anti-Olympic Campaigns' in Lenskyj, H and Wagg, S (eds) *The Palgrave Handbook of Olympic Studies* (Palgrave, Basingstoke), at 534.

6 Cottrell, M P and Nelson, T (2010) 'Not Just the Games? Power, Protest and Politics at the Olympics' 17(4) *European Journal of International Relations* 729–753, at 731.

7 On the local level, for example, see Bourbilleres, H, Gasparini, W and Koebel, M (2021) 'Local protests against the 2024 Olympic Games in European cities: the cases of the Rome, Hamburg, Budapest and Paris bids' *Sport in Society*, https://doi.org/10.1080/17430437.2021.1960312.

8 Dalton, C and Taylor, J (2021) 'Are COVID-19-Safe Tokyo Olympic and Paralympics Really Possible?' 215(2) *Medical Journal of Australia* 54–56.

9 McCurry, J (2021) 'Claims could run into billions': the interests at stake if Olympics in Japan were cancelled' *The Guardian*, 10 June, available at: https://www.theguardian.com/sport/2021/jun/10/claims-could-run-into-billions-the-interests-at-stake-if-olympics-in-japan-were-cancelled (last accessed 27/01/2022).

10 Anderson, J (2021) 'Can the Olympics still be cancelled? Yes but the legal and financial fallout would be staggering' *The Conversation* https://theconversation.com/can-the-olympics-still-be-cancelled-yes-but-the-legal-and-financial-fallout-would-be-staggering-161739 (last accessed 27 January 2022).

11 McElhinney, D (2021) 'Olympic review. Was Tokyo 2020 a success?' available at: https://www.tokyoweekender.com/2021/08/olympic-review-tokyo-2020-success/ (last accessed 27/01/2022).

12 Majumdar, B (2021) 'How Covid changed sport - a case study of the 2020 Tokyo Olympic Games' *Sport in Society* DOI: 10.1080/17430437.2021.1975963.

13 Duigan, M and Mair, J (2021) 'Tokyo's Olympic legacy: Will hosting the Games have benefitted local communities?' *The Conversation* available at: https://theconversation.com/tokyos-olympic-legacy-will-hosting-the-games-have-benefitted-local-communities-165433 (last accessed 27/01/2022).

14 Kageyama, Y (2022) 'Small protests held in Tokyo and Sapporo against 2030 Winter Olympic bid' *Japan Today* available at: https://japantoday.com/category/sports/small-protests-in-tokyo-and-sapporo-against-olympic-bid?comment-order=popular (last accessed 25/11/2022).

15 Segrave, J (1988) 'Towards a Definition of Olympism' in Segrave, J and Chu, D (eds) *The Olympic Games in Transition* (Human Kinetics, Champaign). See also Girginov, V (2010) 'Studying Olympism' in Girginov, V (ed) *The Olympics: A Critical Reader* (Routledge, London), ch 1.

16 Chatziefstathiou, D (2011) 'Paradoxes and Contestations of Olympism in the History of the Modern Olympic Movement' 14(3) *Sport in Society* 332.

17 Geeraert, A and Gauthier, R (2018) 'Out-of-control Olympics: Why the IOC Is Unable to Ensure an Environmentally Sustainable Olympic Games' 20(1) *Journal of Environmental Policy and Planning* 16–30.

18 Macrury, I and Poynter, G (2008) 'The Regeneration Games: Commodities, Gifts and the Economics of London 2012' 25(14) *International Journal of the History of Sport* 2072–2090.

19 Maguire, J, Butler, K, Barnard, S and Golding, P (2008) 'Olympism and Consumption: An Analysis of Advertising in the British Media Coverage of the 2004 Athens Olympic Games' 25 *Sociology of Sport Journal* 167–186.

20 Davidson, J and McDonald, M (2018) 'Rethinking Human Rights: the 2014 Sochi Winter Olympics, LGBT Protections and the Limits of Cosmopolitanism' 37(1) *Leisure Studies* 64–76.

21 James, M and Osborn, G (2014) 'The missing link: the coming out of ambush marketing?' *LawInSport*, 28 January, available at: http://www.lawinsport.com/articles/intellectual-property-law/item/the-missing-link-the-coming-out-of-ambush-marketing#references (last accessed 22/01/2022).

22 Rule 50(2) Olympic Charter is analysed in detail in Chapter 4.

23 Sochi Organising Committee (2014) *Sochi 2014 Candidate City File* available at: https://library.olympics.com/Default/doc/SYRACUSE/57053/sochi-2014-candidate-city-sochi-2014-bid-committee (last accessed 3/11/2022), at 47. For a more detailed discussion of Rule 33, see Chapter 2.

24 The most high-profile of these advocacy groups was the Principle 6 Campaign, available at: https://www.athleteally.org/p6-campaign-continues-make-difference/ (last accessed 23/02/2022).

25 Henry, I (2012) 'The Olympics: Why We Should Value Them' in Lenskyj, H and Wagg, S (eds) *The Palgrave Handbook of Olympic Studies* (Palgrave, Basingstoke), ch 34.

26 See further, Adi A (2014) 'Olympic Humanitarianism: The Fundamental Principles of Olympism' 3 *Journal of Olympic History* 6–15.

27 Available at: https://stillmedab.olympic.org/media/Document%20Library/OlympicOrg/IOC/What-We-Do/Olympic-agenda/Olympic-Agenda-2020-5-15-recommendations.pdf (last accessed 23/02/2022).

28 Olympic Sustainability documents available at: https://olympics.com/ioc/sustainability (last accessed 23/02/2022).

29 IOC Strategic Framework on Human Rights available at: https://stillmed.olympics.com/media/Documents/Beyond-the-Games/Human-Rights/IOC-Strategic-Framework-on-Human-Rights.pdf (last accessed 3/11/2022).

30 Pound, R (2021) 'Olympic Values: Sponsorship, Values and Integrity in Sport Creating as Paradigm Shift' in Chatziefstathiou, D, Garcia, B and Seguin, B (eds) *Routledge Handbook of the Olympic and Paralympic Games* (Routledge, London), ch 7.

31 James, M and Osborn, G (2011) 'London 2012 and the Impact of the UK's Olympic and Paralympic Legislation: Protecting Commerce or Preserving Culture? 74(3) *Modern Law Review* 410–429.

32 Flyvbjerg, B Budzier, B and Lunn, D (2021) 'Regression to the Tail: Why the Olympics Blow Up.' 53(2) *Environment and Planning A: Economy and Space* 233–260.

33 Abel, J (2021) '12th round of Caster Semenya's legal fight: too close to call?' *Asser International Sports Law Blog*, 11 November, available at: https://www.asser.nl/SportsLaw/Blog/?tag=/Caster-Semenya (last accessed 23/02/2022).

34 Geeraert, A and Gauthier, R (2018) 'Out-of-control Olympics: Why the IOC Is Unable to Ensure an Environmentally Sustainable Olympic Games' 20(1) *Journal of Environmental Policy & Planning* 16–30.

35 Boykoff, J (2020) *NOlympians Inside the Fight Against Capitalist Mega-Sports in Los Angeles, Tokyo and Beyond* (Fernwood Publishing, Halifax).

36 See, in particular, Principles 1–4, Preamble, Olympic Charter.

37 See, for example, James, M and Osborn, G (2014) 'The missing link: the coming out of ambush marketing?' *LawInSport*, 28 January, available at: https://www.lawinsport.com/topics/intellectual-property-law/item/the-missing-link-the-coming-out-of-ambush-marketing (last accessed 23/02/2022).

38 Rule 1.2-4 Olympic Charter.

39 Toohey, K and Veal, A (2007) *The Olympic Games: A Social Science Perspective* (CABI, Oxford), 278–279.

40 IOC, *The Olympic Symbols*, available at: https://olympics.com/ioc/olympic-rings (last accessed 02/05/2023). See also Lennartz, K (2001/2) 'The Story of the Rings' 10 *Journal of Olympic History* 29.

41 Available at: http://www.wipo.int/treaties/en/ip/nairobi/ (last accessed 22/01/2022).

42 The exceptional nature of these protections is such that the only other symbols to receive similar legislative protections in the UK are those covered by s6 Geneva Conventions Act 1957, including in particular the Red Cross and Red Crescent.

43 Whilst women did compete in certain events at earlier Games, they were only allowed to compete in the blue riband athletics events from 1928. See more generally Chatziefstathiou, D (2011) 'Paradoxes and Contestations of Olympism in the History of the Modern Olympic Movement' 14(3) *Sport in Society* 332–344.

44 See generally Girginov, V (ed) (2010) *The Olympics. A Critical Reader* (Routledge, London) and Lenskyj, H and Wagg, S eds (2012) *The Palgrave Handbook of Olympic Studies* (Palgrave, Basingstoke).

45 Dyreson, M (2008) 'Epilogue: Athletic Clashes of Civilizations or Bridges over Cultural Divisions? The Olympic Games as Legacies and the Legacies of the Olympic Games' 25(14) *International Journal of the History of Sport* 2117–2129, at 2117.

46 Milton-Smith, J (2002) 'Ethics, the Olympics and the Search for Global Values' 35 *Journal of Business Ethics* 131–142, at 132.

47 Hayes, G and Karamichas, J (2014) 'Conclusion: Sports Mega-events; Disputed Places, Systemic Contradictions and Critical Moments' in Hayes, G and Karamichas (eds) *Olympic Games, Mega-events and Civil Societies* (Palgrave, London), 249–261.

48 James, M and Osborn, G (undated) Agenda 2020: Submission to IOC (copy on file with authors).

49 Tomlinson, A (2006) 'Los Angeles 1984 and 1932: Commercializing the American Dream' in Tomlinson, A and Young, C (eds) *National Identity and Global Sports Events: Culture, Politics and Spectacle in the Olympics and the Football World Cup* (SUNY Press, New York), at 168.

50 Smart, B (2018) 'Consuming Olympism: Consumer Culture, Sport Star Sponsorship and the Commercialisation of the Olympics' 18(2) *Journal of Consumer Culture* 241–260.

51 See, for example, James, M and Osborn, G (2016) 'The Olympics, Transnational Law and Legal Transplants: The International Olympic Committee, Ambush Marketing and Ticket Touting' 36(1) *Legal Studies* 93–110. We have purposely chosen not to cover ambush marketing in this book as we have covered it in depth elsewhere and sought to use other instances to illustrate the concepts and approaches we outline. Ambush marketing does, nevertheless, provide a useful vehicle through which to explore our thesis.

52 James, M and Osborn, G (2014) 'The missing link: the coming out of ambush marketing?' *LawInSport*, 28 January, available at: https://www.lawinsport.com/topics/intellectual-property-law/item/the-missing-link-the-coming-out-of-ambush-marketing (last accessed 23/02/2022).

53 Smart, B (2018) 'Consuming Olympism: Consumer Culture, Sport Star Sponsorship and the Commercialisation of the Olympics' 18(2) *Journal of Consumer Culture* 241–260.

54 Hayes, G and Karamichas, J (2014) 'Conclusion: Sports Mega-events; Disputed Places, Systemic Contradictions and Critical Moments' in Hayes, G and Karamachis (eds) *Olympic Games, Mega-events and Civil Societies* (Palgrave, London), at 249. Tomlinson found that the IOC actually made little reference to legacy until the mid-1980s. Before that it was concerned more with survival and dealing

with various crises, although the language can be seen of 'inheritance of benefits' (Montreal 1976) and 'continuing asset' (Melbourne 1956); the notion of legacy eventually '[d]eveloped as a principle to justify the Olympic phenomenon at a time of crisis and survival, 'legacy' was soon turned into a rhetorical tool that could be used in an encomium to the Olympic movement and its stated ideals of peace and international understanding' in Tomlinson, A (2014) 'Olympic Legacies: Recurrent Rhetoric and Harsh Realities' 9(2) *Contemporary Social Science* 137–158, at 139.

55 Boykoff, J and Fussey, P (2014) London's Shadow Legacies: Security and Activism at the 2012 Olympics' 9(2) *Contemporary Social Science* 253, at 254.
56 Smith, A (2014) 'Leveraging Sport Mega-events: A New Model of Convenient Justification?' 6(1) *Journal of Policy Research in Tourism, Leisure and Events* 15–30.
57 Boykoff, J (2011) 'The Anti Olympics' 67 *New Left Review*, at 41.
58 Lenskyj, H (2012) 'The Case against the Olympic Games: The Buck Stops with the IOC' in Lenskyj, H and Wagg, S (eds) *The Palgrave Handbook of Olympic Studies* (Palgrave, Basingstoke), ch 35.
59 Smart, B (2018) 'Consuming Olympism: Consumer culture, Sport Star Sponsorship and the Commercialisation of the Olympics' 18(2) *Journal of Consumer Culture* 241–260, at 242.
60 IOC (2014) Olympic Agenda 2020 20+20 Recommendations available at https://stillmed.olympic.org/Documents/Olympic_Agenda_2020/Olympic_Agenda_2020-20-20_Recommendations-ENG.pdf (last accessed 27/01/2022). See further on Agenda 2020, MacAloon, J (2016) 'Agenda 2020 and the Olympic Movement' 19(6) *Sport in Society* 767–785.
61 Duval, A (2014) 'Olympic Agenda 2020: Window Dressing or New Beginning' *PlaytheGame* 12 June, available at: https://www.playthegame.org/news/comments/2014/olympic-agenda-2020-window-dressing-or-new-beginning/ (last accessed 27/01/2022).
62 These concepts are unpacked and explored in detail in Chapter 2.
63 Shirinian, Z (2014) '"Pompous" IOC demands led to withdrawal of Oslo 2022 Olympic bid,' 3 October, *Insidethegames*, available at: http://www.insidethegames.biz/articles/1023008/pompous-ioc-demands-led-to-withdrawal-of-oslo-2022-olympic-bid (last accessed 27/01/2022). See further James, M and Osborn, G (2016) 'The Olympics, Transnational Law and Legal Transplants: The International Olympic Committee, Ambush Marketing and Ticket Touting' 36(1) *Legal Studies* 93–110.
64 Rule 2(13) Olympic Charter. See in particular the criticism levelled at Rio 2016 for building the Olympic golf course on an Area of Environmental Protection, https://nextcity.org/daily/entry/rios-olympic-golf-course-will-wipe-out-a-protected-ecological-gem (last accessed 27/01/2022), and at Pyeongchang 2018 for the destruction of a 500-year old primeval forest to make way for the Alpine skiing events, http://www.gamesmonitor.org.uk/node/2228 (last accessed 27/01/2022).
65 See further Schwab, B (2017) '"When We Know Better, We Do Better." Embedding the Human Rights of Players as a Prerequisite to the Legitimacy of Lex Sportiva and Sport's Justice System' 32 *Maryland Journal of International Law* 4, available at: http://digitalcommons.law.umaryland.edu/mjil/vol32/iss1/4 (last accessed 3/05/2022).
66 IOC statement available at: https://www.olympic.org/news/ioc-strengthens-its-stance-in-favour-of-human-rights-and-against-corruption-in-new-host-city-contract (last accessed 27/01/2022).
67 See Chapter 2 for a detailed analysis of the IOC's law-making powers.
68 The impact of these changes is the focus of Chapter 3.
69 The impact and legality of Rule 50(2) Olympic Charter and its Guidance are analysed in Chapter 4.

70 Pound, R (2021) 'Olympic Values: Sponsorship, Values and Integrity in Sport Creating a Paradigm Shift' in Chatziefstathiou, D, García, B and Séguin, B (eds), *Routledge Handbook of the Olympic and Paralympic Games* (Routledge, London), 83.

71 On the accountability of the IOC from a global governance perspective, see Nelson, T and Cottrell, M P (2015) 'Sport without Referees? The Power of the International Olympic Committee and the Social Politics of Accountability' 22(2) *European Journal of International Relations* 1–22.

2 The Curious Case of the IOC and the Creation of Olympic Law

Introduction

Chapter 1 outlined the tensions at the heart of the Olympic Movement and our approach to analysing them. This chapter is also a foundational one, in that it examines the scope and function of the International Olympic Committee (IOC) and its extraordinary legal powers. It begins with an unpacking of the history and context of the IOC, exploring its origins, politics, and reach, before proceeding to examine its curious and ground-breaking law-creating powers. These powers, and the tensions that they create, are explored specifically in Chapters 3 and 4. Here, we examine the overarching tension created by the Olympic legal framework between the failure to require the promotion of the culture of Olympism by law and the explicit requirement that hosts protect the commercial rights associated with the Olympic Games by bespoke legislation. As a result, this chapter adds a further nuance or extension to the approach outlined in Chapter 1. The legal status of the IOC and the ways in which it creates its own legal norms, the *lex Olympica*, are analysed here to demonstrate how this internal law fits within the more general sporting-legal framework of *lex sportiva*. It then discusses the creation of Olympic law, and how this growing body of IOC-driven legislation is reinforced and disseminated to other major sports events through the diffusion and transplantation of the legal frameworks implemented to protect commercial rights vested in the Olympic Movement. Before considering this, however, we turn first to an examination of the history, scope, influence, and legal context of the IOC.

History and context: The International Olympic Committee

The IOC was founded on 23 June 1894. Its genesis owed much to Baron Pierre de Coubertin and the discussions that he had facilitated in the preceding years, with its initial composition very much drawn from those with whom

DOI: 10.4324/9780429323355-2

he had consulted. The original IOC comprised 16 people from 13 nations and was avowedly international in its outlook:

> The international composition reflected Coubertin's universal ambitions with the Olympic movement. He foresaw that the IOC maintained an exclusive group of individuals that self-recruited new members who could contribute to the global development of the Olympic Movement.[1]

Krieger and Wassong chart developments in the history of the governance of the IOC, including ongoing debates as to whether International Sports Federations (ISFs) should have automatic membership of the IOC, the question of age limits for its members, and, in 1968, the need for statutory and thematic commissions to be created because of the increased complexity of staging each edition of the Olympic Games. The latter part of the 20th century saw a continued discussion on the composition of the IOC's membership and related areas of good governance. The key moment for the IOC was, however, the Salt Lake City scandal, which focussed on claims of bribery in the bidding process for the 2002 edition of the Winter Games. The impact of the scandal was dramatic for the IOC,[2] leading to changes in its composition, the powers of the President, and his relationship with the Executive Board. The IOC website currently describes its role and position as being:

> The ... guardian of the Olympic Games and the leader of the Olympic Movement. A truly global organisation, it acts as a catalyst for collaboration between all Olympic stakeholders, including the athletes, the National Olympic Committees, the International Federations, Organising Committees for the Olympic Games, the Worldwide Olympic Partners and Olympic broadcast partners. It also collaborates with public and private authorities including the United Nations and other international organisations. The vision of the International Olympic Committee is to Build a Better World through Sport.[3]

Much of this description, or 'sales puff,' is undeniable and the vision laudable, although contested. Gauthier notes that the IOC's scope broadened as the Games became more commercialised and that legacy and sustainability have become key watchwords since the 1990s.[4] He also argues that the IOC lacks democratic legitimacy, notwithstanding its attempts to make itself more representative. More worrying questions remain about its substantive legitimacy considering its stance on a variety of human rights issues, violations of labour rights, and broader issues of moral responsibility. The most recent IOC reforms come courtesy of Agenda 2020 and the updated Agenda 2020+5.[5] Whilst the scope and purview of these reviews were broad, some of the recommendations focussed on changes to the IOC itself. MacAloon noted that these changes were, however, of little real impact; in effect, they were little more than 'corporate boilerplate' and rather general in nature, such as a broad commitment to comply with good governance principles. These are perfectly credible and laudable steps, '... but unlikely to dent the public image problems from which the organization suffers.'[6]

Of particular importance to the good governance agenda was instigating the targeted recruitment of new IOC members with specific competencies. The Nominations Commission now operates with specific criteria throughout the recruitment process and examines all candidates before presenting their findings to the IOC Executive Board. The Nominations Commission focuses on four criteria: the IOC's needs in terms of skills and knowledge; geographic balance; gender balance; and the existence of an Athlete's Commission within the organisation for representatives of the ISFs and/or the National Olympic Committees (NOCs).[7] The result of these changes is that sporting background and expertise are given greater importance than was the case previously, and the IOC's governance structures now more adequately reflect contemporary expectations.

The Olympic Charter defines the IOC as 'an international non-governmental not-for-profit organisation, of unlimited duration, in the form of an association with the status of a legal person, recognised by the Swiss Federal Council.'[8] Outside of this legalistic definition, the IOC can also be classified objectively as a transnational organisation. The IOC is a large, hierarchically organised and centrally directed enterprise that performs specialised, technical functions across, and in relative disregard of, national boundaries.[9] Although the IOC can be categorised as both an international non-governmental organisation and a transnational organisation, it operates differently from other similar bodies, particularly those that act within the sports sector. It is useful in terms of understanding its wider role to consider the counterfactual of what it is *not*. It is *not* the regulatory body for a specific sport, or family of sports, that governs those subject to its rules via a series of interlocking contractual relationships, as is the case for the vast majority of ISFs.[10] It is *not* a public-private partnership, as is the case with the World Anti-Doping Agency (WADA),[11] and it is *not* a cross-border specialist arbitral body, as is the Court of Arbitration for Sport (CAS).[12] The IOC's role is, instead, to organise the staging of the Olympic Games and to promote the Fundamental Principles of Olympism throughout the world. Although some of its relationships are similar to those of an ISF with its members, such as those with the NOCs and the ISFs themselves, others, in particular those entered into with individual nation states, are unique and sit outside traditional categorisations of a transnational organisation.

The Olympic legal framework and its relationship with *lex sportiva*

To understand the concept of Olympic law, we need first to define *lex Olympica* and identify the key sources of the IOC's norm creating powers. However, before we define *lex Olympica* and Olympic law, we need to explore the somewhat opaque definitions of *lex sportiva* and sports law. There has been a long, and slightly painful, debate about whether sports law exists as a discrete discipline, and in particular whether it can and should be identified as an area of academic study. Siekmann noted that once this question of whether sports law can be considered a substantive area of study is answered,[13] then the next question is to examine its scope and content.

> Whether a cohesive set of rules exists or whether sports law is nothing more than a mosaic arbitrarily constructed from a diversity of generally accepted and separate areas of law - the law of obligations, torts, intellectual property, administrative law - is the subject of continuing debate.[14]

Any attempt to define *lex Olympica* and Olympic law will necessarily begin with an entanglement with the meaning of *lex sportiva* and our understanding of the interactions between sport and the law. The phrase *lex sportiva* has, in particular, been attributed with a variety of, occasionally conflicting, meanings.[15] For example, Mitten and Opie make the valid point that there is no consensus as to the precise ambit and scope of the field,[16] Beloff that the *lex sportiva* question is a perpetual and persistent problematic, and as can be seen below, authors such as Foster, Latty, and Duval have joined the debate applying various theoretical lenses in an attempt to provide clarity. Before we examine these specifically, it should be noted that whilst definitions of *lex sportiva* have been attempted, there is no universally accepted definition of what it should encompass.[17] Even the use of the Latin-inspired phrase has been the subject of criticism, with Siekemann noting that '[t]he term's inscrutability increases its allure, combining the legitimising cachet of Latin with the malleability of obscure concepts such as "lex" and "sport."'[18] Duval raises the further question of whether *lex sportiva* is even a legitimate source of law. He identifies the problem as that:

> In the absence of international rules imposed conjointly by national states, the football world has developed, in the shadow of Bosman and Swiss arbitration law, a specific "global law without the state." A global law which is not the product of a global democracy but of a messy, invisible, political process involving a plurality of actors representing a conflicting set of interests. This obviously raises burning questions of

legitimacy ... To point out the prevalence of this peculiar and influential set of private rules is already an important step in critically engaging with this particular dimension of the problem.[19]

Latty adds:

The law produced by the international sporting bodies (International Olympic Committee, international federations, continental federations etc) in effect constitutes a legal phenomenon similar to the *lex mercatoria* or to religious laws, insofar as these bodies which are private entities - are at the origin of globally or at least extra-nationally - applied rules, designed to govern the system of sporting competition. Thus the neologism "*lex sportiva*" is being increasingly used as a direct reference to the *lex mercatoria*, either to indicate the set of transnational sporting rules, or in a more limited sense, referring only to the case law of the Court of Arbitration for Sport.[20]

Our preferred attempt at a definition and conceptualisation of *lex sportiva* is provided by Foster. Foster suggests calling the combination of arbitration and regulation that has evolved 'global sports law,' something which he sees as a branch, or form, of transnational law. In his 2019 revisiting of his earlier attempts to map the area, and his review of the newer literature on the subject, Foster notes:

All variations of the concept of *lex sportiva* narrow the theoretical scope of inquiry and criticism. They do so in a manner that forecloses the debate by implicitly legitimising the self-created regulatory regime of international sport and its interpretative organs. It is imperative to have a wider interpretation of global sports law so that it encompasses wider constitutional, legislative, and administrative elements.[21]

He explores several different conceptual approaches, specifically that *lex sportiva* could, for example, be seen simply as the individual sports' rules and regulations, or the jurisprudence of CAS, or, more broadly, the normative order of international sports regulation. As he notes above, all of these definitions narrow the scope of inquiry, hence his preference for the use of the term 'global sports law.' For Foster, global sports law is a product of the regulatory regimes of sporting bodies, is a private contractual order, is transnational, and is a *legal order*; in other words, global sports law *is* law.[22] Interestingly, given our approach outlined in Chapter 1 around the tensions at the heart of the Olympic Movement, Foster goes on to argue that any consideration of global sports law shows a further tension between the desire to oust the law and a desire to become law as part of a quest for legitimacy. Contractual authority is an important part of this and when we use *lex sportiva* as a concept, we prefer Foster's conceptualisation, and in particular that these contracts provide the governance framework for sport, something we return to when we discuss *lex Olympica* below. So, for us, *lex sportiva* is the specific framework for governance, regulation, and dispute resolution that is created by the series of interlocking contracts and relationships between ISFs and their key stakeholders. In contrast, sports law is the body of national, international, and translational law that has been enacted specifically to regulate sport, or some aspect or aspects of sport thought to be in need of external regulation. Having outlined the role, scope, and function of the IOC and made some preliminary observations about what we understand to constitute *lex sportiva* and sports law, we now develop a working definition of *lex Olympica*, before examining its relationship to Olympic law.

The creation of *lex Olympica* from the IOC's transnational legal norms[23]

The analysis of the broader concept of the Olympic legal framework is a comparatively underexplored aspect of both transnational sports law and *lex sportiva*.[24] As a private organisation,[25] as opposed to a nation state or international or transnational body created by nation states through treaty provisions, the IOC has no direct law-making capability, nor any formal law enforcement frameworks within which to impose its will. Despite this lack of a formal jurisdiction and consequential direct law-making powers, as a transnational organisation the IOC is a creator of legal norms, the *lex Olympica*, which has much in common in terms of form and application with the more widely applicable *lex sportiva*. What is unusual, however, is that the IOC requires some of this *lex Olympica* to be implemented into the domestic laws of the host nations of each edition of the Olympic Games.[26] This indirect legislative capability is different in both form and scope from the *lex sportiva* that is in general grounded in contract and forms the basis upon which most legal norms are created by ISFs.[27] This 'Olympic law' is the corpus of laws that is created by national, regional, and city legislatures at the express requirement of the IOC as an essential element of hosting the Olympic Games. Failure to do so can, in theory at least, lead to the revocation of the invitation to host the Olympics by the IOC.[28]

   In common with *lex sportiva*, *lex Olympica* is created through the interconnected framework of contractual provisions governing the relationships between the IOC and the key Olympic stakeholders. The power of a body like the IOC to control the Olympic Movement has been likened by Silence to the role of a legislature.[29] Of primary importance in this quasi-legislative framework is the Olympic Charter, of which all members of the Olympic Movement are required to be signatories, whether directly (for example, the ISFs and NOCs) or indirectly (athletes through their participation agreements). The most important of the subsidiary contracts is the Host City Contract (HCC), now the Olympic Host Contract, which governs the relationship between the IOC and the host city, host NOC, and the organising committee of the relevant edition of the Olympic Games.

There has in the past been fundamental disagreement over the scope of *lex Olympica*. International lawyers generally conclude that *lex Olympica* is paramount in defining the processes of international sports law, whereas domestic lawyers are inclined to view the concept as a description of an essentially autonomous body of private law.[30] Where transnational law embraces all legal rules that exceed the framework of a single national legal order, independently of their origin,[31] transnational sports law draws from a similarly wide range of sources, including in particular the private rules of the ISFs and the IOC.[32] *Lex Olympica*, therefore, can be seen as a specific subset of transnational law that provides the normative framework for the Olympic Movement through a series of interlocking contracts. Defined in this way, *lex Olympica* is laid down in the Olympic Charter and everything associated with it, including in particular the HCC, the athlete participation agreement, and the Athletes' Declaration.[33]

The IOC's approach appears to be self-serving; it wants legal protections, but only for itself through the enactment of Olympic law, whilst actively avoiding being subjected to the laws that it doesn't like, such as domestic tax law and international human rights law. This singularity is reinforced by its need to have enacted into law the norms that it has identified as necessary to create the appropriate legal environment within which each edition of the Games can be organised. Without any formal law-making capability, the IOC requires its legal norms to be legislated into existence by the host jurisdiction. Thus, the IOC's lack of a formal legislative capability has a direct impact upon host jurisdictions,[34] by requiring the enactment of the legal guarantees defined in the HCC,[35] which, in turn, results in the creation of Olympic law from *lex Olympica*.

The Olympic Charter as the primary source of *lex Olympica*[36]

The Olympic Charter is the foundational document of *lex Olympica* and stands at the apex of the contractual framework that governs the relationships within the Olympic Movement. Latty states that the *lex Olympica* is the *lex sportiva* originating from the IOC and that the Olympic Charter is located at its core. The Olympic Charter is the overarching constitutional instrument of the Olympic Movement and contains the governing regulatory framework for the IOC itself. Rule 15 of the Olympic Charter states that the IOC is an international non-governmental not-for-profit organisation, of unlimited duration, in the form of an association with the status of a legal person. Its corporate mission, as defined in Rule 2 of the Olympic Charter, is to promote the Fundamental Principles of Olympism throughout the world and to provide leadership for the Olympic Movement.

The Olympic Charter defines the nature and scope of the IOC's relationships with other transnational organisations, such as the ISFs, WADA, and CAS, as well as with the host legislature, city, NOC, and local organising committee. All other sources of *lex Olympica* derive their authority directly from the Olympic Charter, including in particular the HCC. The Olympic Charter is, therefore, seen as having a superior validity by the members of the Olympic Movement.[37]

The Charter also defines the key commercial and intellectual property rights vested in the IOC[38] and the limitations on athletes as individuals to exploit their own commercial rights at the time of the Olympic Games.[39] In stark contrast to this commercial and organisational focus in the Charter's Rules, its preamble contains the Fundamental Principles of Olympism, which act as the underpinning moral grounding of the Olympic Movement and can be equated to its corporate vision or mission statement. The positioning of these Principles in the Preamble is potentially significant as they can be seen as generally applicable interpretative norms that enable an informed interpretation of the substantive regulatory Rules found in the rest of the Charter.[40]

In respect of the host government, though rarely referred to directly,[41] Rule 33(3) of the Olympic Charter requires that:

> The national government of the country of any candidature must submit to the IOC a legally binding instrument by which the said government undertakes and guarantees that the country and its public authorities will comply with and respect the Olympic Charter.

The guarantee is usually provided by means of a covenant entered into by the relevant state authorities and is evidenced in the Candidate City File. For Tokyo 2020, it was covenanted that:

> The Prime Minister of Japan, the Governor of Tokyo and the heads of local authorities related to the hosting of the Tokyo 2020 Olympic and Paralympic Games have all entered into covenants respecting the provisions of the Olympic Charter and the Host City Contract. They fully understand and agree that all commitments made are binding, and they will take all necessary measures to completely fulfil the obligations.[42]

Finally, paragraph G of the HCC states specifically that the IOC enters into the HCC in reliance on the covenant provided by the host government, with clause 66(a)(ii) of the HCC stating specifically that a failure to re-spect the government's covenant gives the IOC the right to terminate the agreement unilaterally.[43] As a result, it appears that the host government is also bound to respect the Olympic Charter. Although having the potential to be extremely powerful if exercised to its fullest by the IOC, this provision appears to be little more than window-dressing. A failure to adhere to the Olympic Charter, including the Fundamental Principles of Olympism, has not been used to justify either a requirement by the IOC of legal change in the host country or to punish hosts whose laws are in conflict with the Charter's requirements.

Technically, the Olympic Charter is the constitution of a private corpora-tion and a contract with its constituent members, although it is considered by some to have a status approaching that of an international treaty.[44] This ena-bles it to occupy a transnational space within which it can create transnational legal norms with little challenge or oversight. Further, the requirement in Rule 33 of the Olympic Charter that the host government sign a legally binding covenant guaranteeing that the host state and its public authorities will comply with and respect the Olympic Charter gives it the aura, if not the status, of an international treaty. The IOC's unique position has resulted in the Olympic Charter being described by Duval as a transnational constitution without a state.[45] Although clearly not a state, the IOC operates, or at least attempts to operate, as much like a state as it can.[46] We return to the desirability of this position in the conclusion.

The Host City Contract as *lex Olympica*

The HCC is the second key source of *lex Olympica*. Rule 36(2) of the Olym-pic Charter states that the HCC 'shall determine the responsibilities of the NOC, the local organising committee and the host concerning the organisa-tion, financing and staging of the Olympic Games as well as the contribution of the IOC to the success of the Olympic Games.' Not only does the HCC define the relationships between the key bodies required to host the Olympic Games, but it also operationalises the Olympic Charter in those relationships.

The HCC is weighted heavily in favour of the IOC. Rather like the music company that offers a contract on its own terms, dictated by it, and almost completely with their own interests at the heart of the agreement, the IOC uses its leverage to exact the terms that it wants from the contractors.[47] Remarkably, it ensures that it receives all of the benefits of the Games taking place, but without the drawback of having to be accountable, particularly in terms of the financial responsibilities if anything goes wrong. Indeed, the financial guarantees acceded to by the host are an increasingly visible and contentious part of the HCC. The insistence on financial guarantees was one of the main reasons why Boston rejected the opportunity to bid for the 2024 Olympic Games. Similarly, the IOC was able to insist on the delayed Tokyo

2020 Games (and Beijing 2022) taking place during a global pandemic, and whilst much of Japan was governed by state of emergency provisions, because a failure to have done so would have left the Japanese hosts massively financially exposed.

The key terms of the HCC are illuminating. The document is extremely one-sided, echoing the 'take it or leave it' approach adopted by parties in the stronger bargaining position. Under clause 66, the IOC can unilaterally terminate the agreement, with no corresponding power vested in the host. The obligations of the host are explained in clause 5, which provides that the host city, local organising committee, and NOC honour and enforce all commitments. The obligations placed upon the host are onerous, whilst those placed on the IOC are minimal by comparison. Indeed, the IOC protects itself further by clause 72, which ensures that it is not affected adversely by any subsequent legal enactments of the host government. This was seen in practice at Tokyo 2020: if the Japanese government had taken steps to prohibit the entry of participants and/or the IOC 'Family' into Japan, the organisers would have been responsible financially for any losses incurred by the Games not taking place, or taking place in a less commercially attractive way. Thus, the HCC facilitates the IOC's imposition of its will, its *lex Olympica*, on the host.

The creation of Olympic law from *lex Olympica*

The transnational legal norms developed by the IOC, the *lex Olympica*, become Olympic law when the host legislature of an edition of the Olympic Games is required to enact specific legislation for the benefit of the IOC and its commercial partners. This process of 'forced law creation' occurs when the law is diffused from one jurisdiction to the next, usually by means of legal transplantation. This process extends the law-making power of the IOC beyond the contractual, where the *lex Olympica* provides the regulatory framework within which an edition of the Olympic Games must be organised, to the municipal or national, through the enactment of bespoke, usually Olympics-specific, legislation. It is this forced creation of, or forced transplantation into, national law in the host jurisdiction that causes Olympic law to fall outside of the usual definitions of both sports law and transnational law, rendering Olympic law a new category of both. It is the body of national laws that is forced into existence by a privately constituted transnational organisation that is seeking to bring to life its transnational legal norms; the IOC is not discharging its duties in cooperation with host jurisdictions,[48] but is compelling them to act on its behalf through the exercise of the leverage it exacts over them.

The compulsion to enact this Olympic law is the combination of the legal guarantees provided in the HCC and the concomitant threat of the removal of the invitation to host the Olympics for failure to comply.[49] Although the relationship between the IOC, local organising committee, host city, and NOC is ostensibly contractual, the reality is that there is no genuine opportunity for negotiation. As was seen in the run-up to the delayed Tokyo 2020 edition, despite scientific and popular opinion supporting a further delay or cancellation of the Games, the IOC insisted that they go ahead, regardless of the risks of exposing athletes, accredited personnel, and the Japanese public to the further spread of Covid-19. The only time that the terms of the relationship are negotiable is where the IOC is unable to exploit its usual degree of leverage because of the lack of potential hosts. This was seen most explicitly in the invitation to Los Angeles to host the 1984 Olympics, when the host city's usual financial underwriting guarantees were waived.

The reasons for nation states acquiescing to these legal guarantees are not entirely straightforward. At its most basic, the legal guarantees required of the host jurisdiction are a term of the HCC. Therefore, if the host jurisdiction's existing laws do not already afford the IOC and the local organising committee the necessary protections and exemptions, then specific laws, such as the London Olympic Games and Paralympic Games Act 2006, must be enacted to discharge the contractual duty to provide those guarantees. In particular, the IOC requires legislation that protects its commercial properties and those of the Games from ambush marketing,[50] including in particular the Olympic symbol, emblem, mascots, and 'CITY + YEAR' designation (for example, Paris 2024).[51] Legislation is also required to ensure that the Olympic venues and their immediate environs are 'clean' so that they are free from sponsorship inside the venues and free from non-official advertising around them.[52] The final element of the commercially restrictive Olympic laws prohibits the unauthorised resale of event tickets ('ticket touting' or 'scalping') and the regulation of street traders. Further legislation covering standard IOC demands including, for example, the provision of income tax exemptions for Olympic accredited personnel,[53] and the creation of dedicated traffic lanes for Olympic vehicles[54] form an integral part of the portfolio of laws that constitute the Olympic law framework. However, when the need for such legislation, and in particular the anti-ambush marketing and ticket touting provisions enacted in the UK in advance of London 2012, was questioned in Parliament, the government's response was simply the truism that the laws had been enacted because the IOC required it.[55] Simply put, if neither existing municipal law nor Olympics-specific law is in place to provide the protections and perks that the IOC requires, then the organisers are in breach of contract and can, in theory at least, have the right to host the Games rescinded.[56]

Whether or not this is more than a mere technical possibility is unknown. The financial, political, and public relations fallouts would make removal of the Games from a host very much an option of last resort. The withdrawal of the Commonwealth Games Federation's invitation to Durban to host the 2022 Commonwealth Games is an extreme example that demonstrates that the use of this ultimate sanction is possible, though perhaps unlikely to be replicated with an Olympic Games. Durban was in breach of a number of the fundamental conditions of its HCC, including in particular that it had failed to appoint an organising committee and that it had been unable to secure the necessary financial guarantees from the national or state governments.[57] However, the threat has been made in respect of Indonesia's hosting of the IOC-sanctioned 2017 Asian Games. After a dispute over the use of the Olympic rings in the insignia of the Indonesian National Sports Council, the IOC stated that only it and the Indonesian Olympic Committee were entitled to use protected Olympic branding. It added that Indonesia would not be considered a suitable host of the Asian Games if it was not capable of protecting the Olympic Properties within its own jurisdiction and that the Olympic Council of Asia would revisit its invitation to host the Games if the dispute was not settled appropriately. As soon as the dispute was settled in favour of the Indonesian Olympic Committee, the threat of revocation was withdrawn.[58]

A further but more nuanced explanation for compliance with the IOC's demands is that whilst bidding cities are faced with pressure to strive for increased uniqueness in their vision for the interpretation of an Olympiad, the reality is that strategic isomorphism leads to the opposite situation where increased homogeneity occurs because of deliberate choices made by candidate cities.[59] As a result, bid documentation tends to exhibit significant similarities of approach to meeting the demands of the IOC in order to be seen as legitimate bidders. Although such an approach could be seen as counterintuitive, as conformity reduces differentiation amongst the rival bidders, the concomitant reduction in risk associated with a bid perceived to be lacking in legitimacy by those engaged with the process of choosing a host can actually increase a bidder's chance of success.[60] In other words, rather than create an unequivocally unique competitive position in the bidding environment, candidate cities will use their resources to gain 'social acceptance resulting from adherence to regulative, normative, or cognitive norms and expectations.'[61] Where the creation of Olympic law is concerned, this tendency results in candidate cities, including the ultimate host, promising to enact as a minimum the same protections as each other, each of which is based on the presumed success of the provisions enacted by predecessor hosts.

The process by which this forced law creation can be best conceptualised is as a form of legal diffusion.[62] When normative and legal orders coexist in the same context of time and space, as is the case with the IOC and the host nation of the Olympics, sustained interaction is inevitable. Diffusion of the law is generally considered to take place when one legal order, system, or tradition influences another in a significant way;[63] here, where the normative frameworks devised by the IOC influence the domestic law of the host nation. One of the most common processes of legal diffusion is the legal transplant,[64] by which the laws of the originator jurisdiction are exported to that of the adopter, with a greater or lesser degree of amendment. There are two elements of exceptionalism where Olympic law is concerned. First, the diffusion observed here does not involve one-way traffic between the national laws of two countries.[65] Instead, the original normative framework is created at the transnational level by a private, transnational, non-state organisation (the IOC), rather than in the domestic law of a nation state, before it becomes law for the first time. Further, before each subsequent diffusion of the relevant laws, the legislation returns to the IOC to be internalised into its own normative framework. Perceived deficiencies are addressed and the laws are updated in accordance with the narrative debriefings provided to the IOC and the Coordination Commission by the immediate past organising committee, before further diffusion to the host jurisdiction of the next edition of the Olympics occurs. Thus, the diffusive effect is more than simply internationalised; it is a transnationalised phenomenon. Secondly, the adopter of the diffused law is forced to create law for the benefit of the IOC and its affiliates, rather than choosing to do so, under threat of having the right to host the Olympics rescinded.

This transnationalised process of legal diffusion, or legal transplantation,[66] resulting in forced law creation is exemplified by the passage of the first iteration of Olympic law to be enacted at Sydney 2000 to the latest version in place for the current Olympiad. The first stage of this process of diffusion is when the norms that originated at the transnational level are required of the host nation's legal system. This results in the legal norms created originally by the IOC, in the guise of the legal guarantees required in the Host City Contract, becoming incorporated into law. This diffusion first became visible in the legislation enacted in New South Wales and Australia to protect the commercial rights associated with Sydney 2000.[67] Following the perceived success of these legislative provisions, the second stage of the process occurs when the host jurisdiction's laws (in this first case of the various Australian jurisdictions) undergo a process of transnationalisation. This transnationalised legal diffusion is performed as the municipal law is returned to the IOC where it influences the development of the IOC's own internal legal norms, the *lex Olympica*. These norms are then recalibrated and extended, resulting in 'legislative creep' by which Olympic law exerts control over an ever-greater range of activities.[68] These requirements are then diffused to the next host, which in turn is forced to internalise the required normative framework once again by the creation of the next iteration of Olympic law.

What is unique about the diffusion and transplantation of Olympic law is not its genesis in a transnational legal space, but the process by which it is effectively 'forced' upon the host. Whereas it is common for a jurisdiction to have its laws influenced by those of others, whether a former colonial power, adherence to norms of best practice, or imposed standardisation across a trading block, Olympic law is forced on a host jurisdiction by the IOC's exercise of the leverage that it holds over prospective hosts. The requirement that these legal frameworks are enacted provides the IOC, albeit indirectly, with the formal law-making capability that it otherwise lacks.

The ultimate expression of such legal diffusion is the pre-emptive enactment by a potential host of generic protective laws, as opposed to the edition-specific legislation that has been enacted for each Olympics since Sydney 2000.[69] The advent of these generic laws effectively provides a compliant legal landscape based upon the likely demands of mega-event owners. They are enacted to enable the potential host to bid for any such event without the need to enact specific legislation on each occasion that an event is successfully secured and, therefore, without the need for such legislative frameworks to be subjected to repeated Parliamentary scrutiny.[70] In this way, Olympic law is developed at the transnational level, but enacted in national legislation; conceived globally but born locally.

Whatever the reasons behind the creation of Olympic law, a particular problem with the legislative process is the comparative lack of Parliamentary scrutiny of the domestic legislation. The enactment of Olympic law is generally a reactive and functional process; it is created because the IOC demands it as a condition of hosting the Games, rather than there being a justifiable, evidence-based need for it. This leads to a self-referentialisation of the creation of Olympic law: it is enacted because the IOC demands it; the IOC demands it because it perceives previous iterations of Olympic law to have been successful; the perception of success comes from the report of the previous organising committee, for whose benefit the law was passed only because the IOC demanded it of its host legislature. Unless or until this diffusive cycle of legislative transplants is broken by either robust Parliamentary debate about the need for the individual laws passed, or by a challenge to their validity in court, the perception that they are working effectively will continue. This self-referentialism is replicated where generic laws are enacted as it is only when the original enabling legislation is enacted that full Parliamentary scrutiny will take place. It is likely that in the face of additional examination by legislatures and courts, some of the laws will remain an integral part of the Olympic legal framework, but it is not guaranteed that all are necessary to the extent that they are currently demanded. What is perhaps more intriguing is that this current approach protects the commercial imperatives of hosting the Games, but not the underlying core principles of Olympism itself, exposing explicitly the tension between the culture of the Olympic Movement and its commercial imperatives.

Conclusion

As we have illustrated, the IOC is a curious and powerful beast and its law-making powers as a private body are ground-breaking. We have explored how the IOC manifests its norms by creating its own version of *lex sportiva*, the *lex Olympica*, and how these are then actualised through transplantation into specific Olympic laws by pliant host states. This process can be observed in two distinct contexts. First in the host itself,[71] where 'state of exception'[72] regulations persist after the conclusion of the Olympic Games,[73] or are re-used elsewhere within the former host to increase the regulation and/or criminalisation of what were previously lawful and/or unregulated behaviours.[74] The term 'state of exception' was coined by Agamben and broadly denotes a technique adopted by a government or state, effectively creating a voluntary state of emergency.[75] The transformation of the spatial and legal landscape for an edition of the Olympic Games is arguably an unofficial declaration of a state of exception, providing the host with a range of extraordinary powers,[76] positioning mega events such as the Olympics as both literal and figurative sites of legal exceptionalism.[77]

The second context in which this process can be seen is in the genesis of this legislation. We demonstrate how the laws promulgated by subsequent hosts of the Olympic Games, and other sporting mega events that incorporate earlier iterations of Olympic law into their domestic legal systems,[78] or where potential hosts introduce similar statutory provisions pre-emptively as a means of demonstrating the legitimacy of a bid to the wider Olympic Movement,[79] operate to provide the IOC with wide-ranging, but indirect, law-making powers. This latter phenomenon reaches its apotheosis where jurisdictions that have developed a strategic plan to attract major sporting events introduce generic legislation that complies in advance with the demands made by organisations such as the IOC.

We now proceed to examine examples of the operation of the Olympic legal framework in practice. The chapter has illustrated how Olympic law reinforces the tension we outlined in Chapter 1. Our overarching argument is that the IOC needs to recalibrate its approach to what it requires of its hosts and stakeholders, to utilise its leverage more strategically to create a more apposite balance between the protection of its income streams and the promotion of Olympism. We develop this further in the following chapters with an examination of two specific case studies. We begin with a consideration of the legality of Rule 40 of the Olympic Charter, which attempts to regulate the ability of an athlete to use their image, performance at, and participation in an edition of the Games for their own commercial advantage. We then move on to analyse the legality and human rights implications of the prohibition on athlete activism in Rule 50(2) of the Olympic Charter. Whilst analyses of these issues have occurred in more mainstream commentaries, the very direction and focus of the Olympic Movement has come under increasing scrutiny. Forceful arguments have been made highlighting that the IOC has privileged commercial imperatives over what is supposed to be an overarching Olympic philosophy and regulatory approach.[80] The need to rebalance this position underpins some of the key strands of the Agenda 2020 developments,[81] and it will be argued that the role of the law in reinforcing this rebalancing is key.

Notes

1 Krieger, J and Wassong, S (2021) 'The Composition of the IOC' in Chatziefstathiou, D, Garcia, B and Seguin, B (eds) *Routledge Handbook of the Olympic and Paralympic Games* (Routledge, London), at 204.

2 See Krieger, J and Wassong, S (2021) 'The Composition of the IOC' in Chatziefstathiou, D, Garcia, B and Seguin, B (eds) *Routledge Handbook of the Olympic and Paralympic Games* (Routledge, London), at 210–212.

3 IOC (2021) Official website https://olympics.com/ioc/overview (last accessed 22/02/2023). See also Rules 1–6 of the Olympic Charter (2021).

4 See Gauthier, R (2016) *The International Olympic Committee, Law, and Accountability* (Routledge, London), ch 8.

5 See Olympic Agenda 2020 + 5, available at: https://olympics.com/ioc/olympic-agenda-2020-plus-5 (last accessed 22/02/2023).

6 MacAloon, J (2016) 'Agenda 2020 and the Olympic Movement' 19(6) *Sport in Society* 767.

7 Krieger, J and Wassong, S (2021) 'The Composition of the IOC' in Chatziefstathiou, D, Garcia, B and Seguin, B (eds) *Routledge Handbook of the Olympic and Paralympic Games* (Routledge, London), at 212.

8 Rule 15(1) of the Olympic Charter (2021).

9 See further Cantelon, H and Letters, M (2000) 'The Making of the IOC Environmental Policy as the Third Dimension of the Olympic Movement' 35(3) *International Review for the Sociology of Sport* 294–308; Macintosh, D and Hawes, M (1992) 'The IOC and the World of Interdependence' 1 *Olympika: International Journal of Olympic Studies* 29–45, at 35; and de Swann, A (1994) *Social Policy beyond Borders: The Social Question in Transnational Perspective* (Amsterdam University Press, Amsterdam).

10 Sugden, J and Tomlinson, A (1998) 'Power and Resistance in the Governance of World Football: Theorizing FIFA's Transnational Impact' 22(3) *Journal of Sport and Social Issues* 299–316.

11 Casini, L (2009) 'Global Hybrid Public–Private Bodies: The World Anti-Doping Agency' 6(2) *International Organisations Law Review* 421–446.

12 On the role of the Court of Arbitration for Sport, see Blackshaw, I (ed) (2006), *The Court of Arbitration for Sport 1984–2004* (TMC Asser Press, The Hague).

13 See also Davis, T (2001) 'What Is Sports Law' 11(2) *Marquette Sports Law Review* 211–244.

14 Siekmann, R (2011) 'What is Sports Law? Lex sportiva and lex Ludica: A Reassessment of Content and Terminology' 11(3–4) *International Sports Law Journal* 3–13, at 4.

15 See in particular, Siekmann, R and Soek, J (2012) *Lex Sportiva: What is Sports Law?* (TMC Asser Press, The Hague) and Foster, K (2016) 'Lex Sportiva and Lex Ludica: The Court of Arbitration for Sport's Jurisprudence' 3(2) *Entertainment and Sports Law Journal* 2.

16 Mitten, M and Opie, H (2010) 'Sports Law: Implications for the Development of International, Comparative and National Law, and Global Dispute *Resolution*' 85 *Tulane Law Review* 269–322.

17 Nafzinger, J (2004) 'Lex sportiva' 3(1–2) *International Journal of Sports Law* 3–7. See also Casini, L and de Oliveira, L V P (2017) '*Lex sportiva* as the Contractual Governing Law' 17 *International Sports Law Journal* 101–116.

18 Siekmann, R (2011) 'What is Sports Law? Lex sportiva and lex Ludica: A Reassessment of Content and Terminology' 11(3–4) *International Sports Law Journal* 3–13, at 6.

19 Duval, A (2016) 'The FIFA Regulations on the Status and Transfer of Players: Transnational Law Making in the Shadow of Bosman' in Duval, A and van Rompuy, B (eds) *The Legacy of Bosman* (TMC Asser Press, The Hague), ch 5.

20 Latty, F (2011) 'Transnational Sports Law' 11(1–2) *International Sports Law Journal* 34–38, at 37.

21 Foster, K (2019) 'Global Sports Law Revisited' 17(1) *Entertainment and Sports Law Journal* 4, https://doi.org/10.16997/eslj.228

22 See Foster, K (2019) 'Global Sports Law Revisited' 17(1) *Entertainment and Sports Law Journal* 4, https://doi.org/10.16997/eslj.228. See also Foster, K (2003) 'Is There a Global Sports Law?' 2(1) *Entertainment Law* 1–18. A close reading of all of Foster's work is essential for any serious sports law scholar. He has variously been described as the 'godfather' of UK sports law and his work has been seen as of 'central importance.' Boyes, S (2019) 'Ken Foster and the Genesis of Sports Law: A Personal Perspective' 17(1) *Entertainment and Sports Law Journal* 3, https://doi.org/10.16997/eslj.225

23 For a detailed analysis of the transnational status of the IOC and its law-making activities, see James, M and Osborn, G (2016) 'The Olympics, Transnational Law and Legal Transplants: The International Olympic Committee, Ambush Marketing and Ticket Touting' 36(1) *Legal Studies* 93–110.

24 Notable exceptions include Maestre, A (2009) *The Law of the Olympic Games* (TMC Asser Press, The Hague); Latty, F (2007) *La lex sportiva: recherche sur le droit transnational* (Martinus Nijhoff, Leiden) and (2001) *Le Comité International Olympique et le Droit International*, (Montchrestien); and Duval, A (2013) 'Lex Sportiva: A Playground for Transnational Law' 19(6) *European Law Journal* 822–842.

25 Rule 15(1) of the Olympic Charter (2015), available at: https://stillmed.olympic.org/Documents/olympic_charter_en.pdf (last accessed 10/08/2016), discussed further below.

26 See further James, M and Osborn, G (2016) 'The Olympics, Transnational Law and Legal Transplants: The International Olympic Committee, Ambush Marketing and Ticket Touting' 36(1) *Legal Studies* 93–110.

27 Foster, K (2003) 'Is There a Global Sports Law?' 2(1) *Entertainment Law* 1, and more generally on the various interpretations of *lex sportiva*, Siekmann, R and Soel, J (eds) (2012) *Lex sportiva: What Is Sports Law?* (TMC Asser Press, The Hague).

28 Rule 36(2) of the Olympic Charter (2021) and further below.

29 Silence, L (1971) 'Les règles du Comité International Olympique et le droit' 50–51 *Revue Olympique* 586–596.

30 Siekmann, R (2011) 'What is Sports Law? Lex Sportiva and lex Ludica: A Reassessment of Content and Terminology' 11(3–4) *International Sports Law Journal* 3–13.

31 Duval, A 'Lex Sportiva: A Playground for Transnational Law' 19(6) *European Law Journal* 822–842, at 836. Duval calls it being agnostic to its source.

32 Latty, F (2011) 'Transnational Sports Latty' 11(1–2) *International Sports Law Journal* 34–38, at 35.

33 See Maestre, A (2009) *The Law of the Olympic Games* (TMC Asser Press, The Hague). The Olympic Charter, Host City Contract, and their relevance to athlete participant agreement and athlete declaration are discussed in Chapters 3 and 4, respectively.

34 Campbell, R (2013) 'Specifying the Global Character of Sports Authority' 2 *Public Diplomacy Magazine* 17.

35 For the relevant parts of the London 2012 agreement, see Clauses 40–42 Host City Contract, available at www.gamesmonitor.org.uk/files/Host%20City%20Contract.pdf (last accessed 22/02/2023).

36 A more detailed analysis of this part of the chapter is provided in James, M and Osborn, G (2023, forthcoming) 'The Influence of European Legal Culture on the Evolution of *Lex Olympica* and Olympic Law' in Duval, A, Krüger, A and Lindholm, J (eds) *The Europeanisation of Lex Sportiva: How European Law Shapes the Governance of Global Sports* (Hart, Oxford).

37 Duval, A (2018) 'The Olympic Charter: A Transnational Constitution without a State?' *Journal of Law and Society* 245–269, at 251.
38 Rules 7–14 of the Olympic Charter (2021).
39 Rule 40 of the Olympic Charter. See further the historical guidance issued by the British Olympic Association, available at: https://www.teamgb.com/docs/default-source/default-document-library/default-document-library/rule-40-guidelines-final.pdf?sfvrsn=2 (last accessed 10/08/2016) and by the United States Olympic Committee, available at: http://www.teamusa.org/Athlete-Resources/Athlete-Marketing/Rule-40-Guidance (last accessed 10/08/2016).
40 Duval, A (2018) 'The Olympic Charter: A Transnational Constitution without a State?' *Journal of Law and Society* 245–269, at 253.
41 Gauthier, R (2016) 'Olympic Game Host Selection and the Law: A Qualitative Analysis' 23 *Jeffrey S. Moorad Sports Law Journal* 1, at 67, available at: https://digitalcommons.law.villanova.edu/mslj/vol23/iss1/1 (last accessed 22/02/2023).
42 Tokyo 2020 Olympic Games Bid Committee, 'Tokyo 2020: Discover Tomorrow,' Section 4.1 Fulfilment of Obligations under the Olympic Charter and Host City Contract, 38, available at: https://library.olympics.com/Default/doc/SYRACUSE/70447/tokyo-2020-discover-tomorrow-tokyo-2020-olympic-games-bid-committee (last accessed 7/11/2022).
43 Copies of the Tokyo 2020 HCC are available at: https://www.2020games.metro.tokyo.lg.jp/eng/taikaijyunbi/taikai/hcc/index.html#:~:text=The%20contract%20between%20the%20Tokyo,in%20Buenos%20Aires%20in%202013 (last accessed 7/11/2022).
44 Maestre, A (2007) 'The Legal Basis of the Olympic Charter' 6(1–2) *International Sports Law Journal* 100–102.
45 Duval, A (2018) 'The Olympic Charter: A Transnational Constitution without a State?' *Journal of Law and Society* 245–269.
46 On the changing nature of the IOC's approach to governance, see Chappelet, J-L (2012) 'From Daily Management to High Politics: The Governance of the International Olympic Committee' in Robinson, L Chelladurai, P Bodet, G and Downward, P (eds), *Routledge Handbook of Sport Management* (Taylor & Francis Group, London).
47 *Schroeder v Macaulay* [1974] 3 All ER 616, per Lord Doplock.
48 Hobe, S (1997) 'Global Challenges to Statehood' 5(1) *Indiana Journal of Global Legal Studies* 191–209, at 196.
49 Rule 36(2) of the Olympic Charter (2021).
50 London Olympic Games and Paralympic Games Act 2006 section 33 and Schedule 4.
51 Clause 41 Host City Contract, available at www.gamesmonitor.org.uk/files/Host%20City%20Contract.pdf (last accessed 22/02/2023).
52 London Olympic Games and Paralympic Games Act 2006 sections 19-21 and London Olympic Games and Paralympic Games (Advertising and Trading) (England) Regulations 2011/2898.
53 London Olympic Games and Paralympic Games Tax Regulations 2010/2913. Under Reg. 5, the list of people who were not ordinarily resident in the UK and thereby capable of claiming tax exempt status under the Regulations included: competitors; media workers; representatives of governing bodies and the IOC; service technicians; team officials; technical officials.
54 Olympic Route Network Designation Order 2009/1573.
55 Lord Davies of Oldham, HL Deb, 11 January 2006, c249. See also the general House of Commons debate at HC Deb, col 208, 21 March 2006, where the scope of, but not the need for, these provisions is discussed. The need for the Olympic-specific legislation is attributed solely to the demands of the IOC as defined in the Host City Contract.

56 Rule 36(2) of the Olympic Charter (2021).
57 Mackay, D. (2017) 'CGF confirms Durban have been stripped of 2022 Commonwealth Games' available at: http://www.insidethegames.biz/articles/1048046/
exclusive-cgf-confirms-durban-have-been-stripped-of-2022-commonwealth-
games (last accessed 22/02/2023).
58 See further http://www.thejakartapost.com/news/2015/02/12/indonesia-row-over-
olympics-logo.html (last accessed 22/02/2023).
59 York, K M and Miree, C. (2015) 'A Longitudinal Exploration of Strategic Isomorphism: The Case of the National Football League' 4(2) *American Journal of
Business and Management* 61–70, at 61. Strategic isomorphism is a term used in
institutional theory to denote the adoption of similar structures and approaches
as other organisations in its environment. Arguably strategic isomorphism is both
a state and a process and it has been argued that a consequence of isomorphism
is organisational legitimacy. There is a broad literature, but see Deephouse, D
(1996) 'Does Isomorphism Legitimate?' 39(4) *Academy of Management Journal*
1024–1039.
60 Fernández-Alles, M and Valle-Cabrera, R (2006) 'Reconciling Institutional Theory
with Organizational Theories' 19(4) *Journal of Organizational Change Management* 503–517, at 505.
61 Deephouse, D and Carter, S (2005) 'An Examination of Differences between Organizational Legitimacy and Organizational Reputation' 42(2) *Journal of Management Studies* 329–360, at 332.
62 Diffusion is used here as the overarching general term, of which there are many
more nuanced variations. For a review of this field of study, see in particular Twining, W (2004) 'Diffusion of Law: A global Perspective' 49 *Journal of Legal Pluralism* 1–45 and its sequel, (2005) 'Social Science and Diffusion of Law' 32(2)
Journal of Law and Society 203–240.
63 Twining, W (2004) 'Diffusion of Law: A Global Perspective' 49 *Journal of Legal
Pluralism* 1–45, at 14.
64 Contrast the approaches of Kahn-Freund, O (1974) 'On Uses and Misuses of Comparative Law' 37 *Modern Law Review* 1–27 and Watson, A (1976) 'Legal Transplants and Law Reform' 92 *Law Quarterly Review* 79–84.
65 Twining, W. (2005) 'Social Science and Diffusion of Law' 32(2) *Journal of Law
and Society* 203–240, at 207.
66 Dolidze, A (2015) 'Bridging Comparative and International Law: Amicus Curiae
Participation as a Vertical Legal Transplant' 26(4) *European Journal of International Law* 851–880.
67 NSW State Environmental Planning Policy No 38 – Olympic Games and Related
Projects, Regulation 11C and the Sydney 2000 Games (Indicia and Images) Protection Act 1996.
68 For further discussion of legislative creep, see James, M and Osborn, G (2016)
'The Olympics, Transnational Law and Tegal Transplants: The International
Olympic Committee, Ambush Marketing and Ticket Touting' 36(1) *Legal Studies*
93–110 and Johnson, P (2008) 'Look Out! It's an Ambush!' 7(2–3) *International
Sports Law Review* 24–29, at 27.
69 The most recent of which are the Rio 2016 laws: Rio 2016 Organising Committee
for the Olympic and Paralympic Games, *Brand Protection Guidelines: Advertising
Market and Advertisers* (version 2, 2014), ch 9, available at: https://library.olym-
pics.com/Default/doc/SYRACUSE/76211/brand-protection-guidelines-advertis-
ing-market-and-advertisers-organising-committee-for-the-olympic-?_lg=en-GB
(last accessed 22/02/2023).
70 For example, New Zealand's Major Events Management Act 2007 and Australia's
Major Sporting Events (Indicia and Images) Protection Act 2014.

71 Dolidze, A (2015) 'Bridging Comparative and International Law: Amicus Curiae Participation as a Vertical Legal Transplant' 26(4) *European Journal of International Law* 851–880.

72 Boykoff, J (2014) *Celebration Capitalism and the Olympic Games* (Routledge, London).

73 For example, the legislation and accompanying technology that was introduced to protect Rio 2016 from acts of terrorism has been left in place indefinitely: Vocativ, 'The Rio Olympics' legacy is a cyber-surveillance state' available at: http://www.vocativ.com/352054/the-rio-olympics-legacy-is-a-cyber-surveillance-state/ (last accessed 6/02/2022).

74 For example, usage of The Royal Parks, some of which host Olympic Fan Zones, is now regulated much more explicitly. On the specific post-London 2012 impact on Hyde Park, see Osborn, G and Smith, A (2015) 'Olympic Brandscapes: London 2012 and the Seeping Commercialisation of Public Space' in Poynter, G, Viehoff, V and Li, Y (eds) *The London Olympics and Urban Development: The Mega-Event City* (Routledge, London), 139–153.

75 Agamben, G (2005) *State of Exception* (CUP, Chicago).

76 See Marrero-Guillamon, I (2012) 'Olympic State of Exception' in Powell, H and Marrero-Guillamon, I (eds), *The Art of Dissent: Adventures in London's Olympic State* (Marshgate Press, London), 20–29. See also Gray, N and Porter, L (2015), 'By Any Means Necessary: Urban Regeneration and the "State of Exception" on Glasgow's Commonwealth Games 2014' 47(2) *Antipode* 380–400.

77 Carrarino, M (2014) 'Law Exclusion Zones: Mega-Events as Sites of Procedural and Substantive Human Rights Violations' XVII *Yale Human Rights and Development Law Journal* 180–204.

78 For example, the Glasgow Commonwealth Games in 2014 utilised the London Olympic Games and Paralympic Games Act 2006 as a template to create a very similar legal framework for the regulation of commercial issues through the enactment of the Glasgow Commonwealth Games Act 2008. See further James, M and Osborn, G (2016) 'The Olympics, Transnational Law and Legal Transplants: The International Olympic Committee, Ambush Marketing and Ticket Touting' 36(1) *Legal Studies* 93–110.

79 York, K M and Miree, C (2015) 'A Longitudinal Exploration of Strategic Isomorphism: The Case of the National Football League' 4(2) *American Journal of Business and Management* 61–70.

80 See James, M and Osborn, G (2011) 'London 2012 and the Impact of the UK's Olympic and Paralympic Legislation: Protecting Commerce or Preserving Culture?' 74(3) *Modern Law Review* 410–429.

81 Agenda 2020 is IOC President Thomas Bach's vision for the reshaping of the Olympic project and is discussed in more depth below. For full details on the IOC's Agenda 2020 proposals, their acceptance, and implementation plans, see https://www.olympic.org/olympic-agenda-2020 (last accessed 22/02/2023).

3 Income and Earnings at the Olympic Games

Introduction

Our analysis so far has identified the key sources of *lex Olympica* and Olympic Law and the tensions that exist between their operationalisation and the Fundamental Principles of Olympism. Central to this analysis is the working conclusion that the extensive law-making powers and, arguably unwarranted, indirect legislative capacity exhibited by the International Olympic Committee (IOC) have resulted in an overarching tension between the underpinning culture and values of the Olympic Movement, Olympism, and what the IOC perceives as a need to maximise the income from its commercial revenue streams.

The impact of IOC's direct law-making capability through the *lex Olympica* has a range of specific impacts on the wider Olympic Movement and, in particular, on the athlete-participants at the Olympic Games. In this and the following chapter, case studies focussing on Rules 40 and 50 of the Olympic Charter examine how the imposition of *lex Olympica* on athletes confirms the existence of the overarching culture-commerce tension through a series of sub-tensions.

In this chapter, the impact of Rule 40(3) of the Olympic Charter (Rule 40), which affects athletes' ability to maximise their commercial opportunities at the Olympic Games, is examined. Explicitly, this chapter illustrates a specific instance of the tension we introduced in the introductory chapter, one that identifies two specific iterations of the culture-commerce tension. First, the tension between the IOC using *lex Olympica* in conjunction with Olympic law as a means of maximising its own commercial revenue, whilst simultaneously imposing restrictions on the athletes that prevent them from generating income from their own participation in the Olympic Games. And, secondly, tension between the IOC's creation of *lex Olympica* and its legality under national and European Union law (EU law).

Using the commercial restrictions imposed on athletes by Rule 40 as an example, it will be demonstrated how *lex Olympica*, particularly its primary form as defined in the Olympic Charter, is imposed on all Olympic stakeholders.

DOI: 10.4324/9780429323355-3

Ostensibly, this is to ensure that the Fundamental Principles of Olympism are adhered to by all signatories of the Olympic Charter. However, the reality is that these restrictions are in place to ensure that the commercial rights of the IOC and the local organising committees of the Olympic Games are protected from any potential economic rivals, including the athletes themselves.

The analysis of Rule 40 will demonstrate how *lex Olympica* has moved from being an unquestioned internal and/or private contractual requirement imposed on athletes, a binding law that was assumed to have some sort of immunity from suit, to a position where it was challenged successfully and found to be unlawful under both German and EU law. This change was instituted *by* athletes and *for* athletes and has resulted in a dilution of the power of the IOC to dictate its commercial terms to its key stakeholders. Further, it demonstrates how litigation underpinned by athlete activism can lead to significant changes in the definition, interpretation, and application of *lex Olympica*.

Before the specifics of Rule 40 are analysed, this chapter situates the analysis in its historical context. In particular, it explores the long-standing requirement that all Olympic athletes had to be amateurs, and in fact they are still prohibited from being directly rewarded financially for their participation in the Games,[1] and the tension that this causes. Having defined the perceived need for, and purview of, Rule 40, we critically examine how it has been operationalised and the legality of its impact on Olympic athletes.

Olympians and earnings: Amateurism in an era of sponsorship and branding

It is somewhat trite to note that elite sport is no longer a pastime but a business.[2] At the very least, elite sport now has economic and commercial dimensions, alongside of its more traditional sporting, educational, and cultural aspects. As Slack notes, 'sport cultures are unavoidably – indeed dialectically – linked to contemporaneous economic, political, social and technological arrangements,'[3] and the commercial dimensions of the sports industry bisect each of these. Sport has become a significant global industry and commoditised market.[4] As a result, sports have altered and adapted their commercial strategies to reflect changing times.

On a macro level, there have been significant sponsorship and advertising gains made in professional sport, with the Olympics at the forefront of many innovative practices.[5] Meanwhile, on a micro level, athletes' contracts have evolved to embrace image rights and personal branding initiatives.[6] Greenfield and Osborn note, with respect to football in particular, that with this increased commercialisation comes greater and more diverse forms of regulation,[7] and it is evident that the increased economic imperatives associated with hosting the Olympics have magnified and accelerated the rights protections and legal frameworks regulating advertising and sponsorship at and around the Games.[8] Indeed, there is now a symbiotic relationship between elite sport and sponsorship, with sports sponsorship defined as '[an] investment, in cash or kind, in an activity in return for access to the exploitable commercial potential associated with that activity.'[9]

The modern Olympic Games are supposed to be a celebration of the aesthetic of sport, of sport as culture and education, and of sport for the sake of sport. To ensure that the Games were not tainted by those who engaged in sport for payment or as part of their employment, all participants in the Olympics had, historically, to be amateur.[10] This in turn created a very specific tension: the IOC and the local organising committee needed to exploit the participation of amateur athletes to be able to generate sufficient income to host the Games. Although International Sports Federations (ISFs) have been allowed to invite professional athletes to compete in their events since Seoul 1988, it is still not accepted as appropriate that athletes monetise their participation in the Olympic Games for their own benefit, as opposed to the benefit of the IOC, the local organising committee, and the Olympic sponsors. Thus, in theory, athletes cannot be paid to participate in the Games and there are no financial rewards paid directly to Olympians.

Rule 40 imposed further specific restrictions on athletes engaging in advertising campaigns for non-official brands:

> Rule 40(3) Except as permitted by the IOC Executive Board, no competitor, coach, trainer or official who participates in the Olympic Games may allow his person, name, picture or sports performances to be used for advertising purposes during the Olympic Games.

> Rule 40(4) The entry or participation of a competitor in the Olympic Games shall not be conditional on any financial consideration.

As challenges were mooted, Rule 40 and the guidance issued by individual National Olympic Committees (NOCs) were relaxed slightly, but not enough to satisfy the growing demand of athletes that they be allowed to earn a living from playing sport. Many Olympic athletes are reliant on their personal sponsors to supply them with kit and to pay them enough of an income to cover their living and participation expenses. For example, Nick Symonds, a longtime advocate of athletes' rights, has argued that without the benefit of his personal sponsors, he would not be able to compete as a full-time athlete. If he was unable to compete full-time, he would have no chance of qualifying for major track and field events, including the Olympics. If his personal sponsors were unable to recognise his achievements, and he was unable to reciprocate by recognising the importance of their support, then personal sponsorships would no longer be commercially viable and the pool of athletes would be diminished. This line of reasoning underpinned his and his sponsor's legal action against USA Track and Field.[11] This clearly illustrates the tension between the IOC's need, and the need of national governing bodies and NOCs, to generate sufficient income to operate effectively, and the athletes' need to earn a living.

Whilst athletes have been seeking ways to recognise the support of their personal sponsors, the Olympic Games has continued to grow as an event. This gigantism needs to be funded to provide the spectacle that is wanted, perhaps even needed, by the IOC, its sponsors, and consumers around the world. The majority of the funding for the Olympic Games is now provided by exclusive broadcasting arrangements and sponsorship deals. These ensure that the commercial rights vested in the IOC and the local organising committee can be exploited effectively, efficiently, and to their fullest. To protect these income streams, and indeed the spaces in which the Games take place, the IOC has pursued a range of strategies to prevent anyone else, including the athletes, from gaining financially directly from the Olympics.

The 1980s saw a step change in the way that the IOC managed its commercial rights. First, it began the process of taking over the negotiation of broadcast contracts for each edition of the Games from the local organising committees.[12] Having established itself as the primary negotiating partner, the IOC was able to develop the Olympics into a desirable global brand, with television proving to be crucial to the commercialisation of the Games.[13] The increased use of exclusive broadcasting arrangements in key markets, such as the USA, the UK, and Germany, ensured a regular income for the IOC on a variety of platforms with which sponsors wanted to be associated.[14] This long-term Olympic broadcasting strategy is designed to ensure the ongoing financial security of the Olympic Movement and of the Olympic Games,[15] with the broadcasts of the Games acting as the main driver of its continued global popularity.

Secondly, the IOC began a similar process of coordinating the international marketing programme for the Olympics, which resulted in the creation of The Olympic Partner Programme (the TOP Programme).[16] The TOP Programme enabled prospective sponsors to negotiate with a single partner, the IOC, to secure exclusive marketing rights in industry-specific categories on a global basis, and to be associated with what they saw as the positive values of Olympism. The success of the TOP Programme has increased the IOC's annual income to well over $1.7bn per year and enabled prestigious global brands to create marketing associations with companies of similar global stature: to be a TOP sponsor 'is to be seen to be moving in world-class company.'[17] The income generated by the broadcasting and marketing arrangements is distributed to the IOC, local organising committees, NOCs, ISFs, and Olympic Solidarity, though with only 0.5% of this income going directly to the athletes who are responsible for generating it. Rule 40 was introduced to protect these revenue streams and, to a certain extent, encourage athlete participation in the advertising campaigns of the TOP sponsors.[18]

Alongside of this strategic repositioning of Olympic broadcasting and marketing has been the introduction of Olympic laws to provide additional protection for the Olympic Properties, as defined in Rules 7–14 of the Olympic Charter. These included the prohibition of unauthorised associations with the Olympic Games and ambush marketing. These legislative protections are available at the international level through the World Intellectual Property Organisation's Nairobi Treaty on the Protection of the Olympic Symbol 1981 and at a domestic level in many countries through bespoke Olympics-specific legislation.[19] In addition, there is an emerging trend of using generic legislation with the potential to provide protections to any major sporting event.[20] These legislative protections are designed to protect the iconography of the IOC and the Olympic Games through the creation of event-specific association rights.[21] This protection is afforded by creating laws that curtail the practice of ambush marketing and whilst not the specific focus of this chapter, this concept is discussed briefly below to provide a contextual understanding.

Ambush marketing is a highly contested term. In his typology of ambush marketing, Nufer identifies 21 different ways in which an ambush can take place, demonstrating the extreme difficulty in trying to develop a universally acceptable overarching definition.[22] One of the more concise definitions describes ambush marketing as '[the] practice whereby another company, often a competitor, intrudes upon public attention surrounding the event, thereby deflecting attention toward themselves and away from the [official] sponsor.'[23] In other words, it is where a non-sponsor tries to exploit the natural interest in an event for their own commercial gain, without paying the sponsorship fee that would enable them to become official sponsors. For their part, the IOC 'characterizes ambush marketing as any intentional or unintentional attempt to create an unauthorized commercial association with the Games that is available only to official sponsors.'[24]

In general, ambush marketing is often thought of as being practised by rival brands operating in the same sector or by regular outsider brands such as Nike and Paddy Power. This is what the legislation, the Olympic law required of a host city, is designed to try and stop. What has become apparent is that it is very difficult to regulate ambush marketing using the law.[25] As a result of this difficulty, personal sponsors have begun to use athletes as sites of both traditional sponsorship and advertising, and ambush marketing strategies. Thus, it is equally possible for athletes to undermine the exclusive sponsorship arrangements of the IOC, local organising committee, and their own NOC by downplaying official brands to protect their personal sponsorships (for example, Michael Jordan's attempt to undermine Reebok's sponsorship of Team USA as he was a Nike athlete) or simply being involved in the promotion of non-official brands (for example, the promotion of Kate Grace by Oiselle).[26]

Athlete commercialisation as an ambush marketing strategy is intrusive of the event and obtrusive in terms of ongoing advertising campaigns running at the same time as the event is taking place.[27] Meanwhile, the IOC has attempted to claim ownership of all aspects of the publicity associated with the Olympics and to restrict opportunities for non-sponsors to deflect the public's attention towards themselves during the Olympic blackout period (the period of time during which Rule 40 was operative). Rule 40 has subsequently become a key provision in the IOC's general approach to combatting ambush marketing by restricting athletes' ability to profit from their appearance at the Olympics through the exploitation of their name, image, and likeness by non-sponsors.

Taken as a whole, these strategies ensure that the physical spaces in which the Olympics are celebrated, including their environs and fan zones,[28] are reconfigured during the Games period and can have an influence for a significant future period. Olympic cities themselves can be seen as 'brandscapes' where entire urban areas, not just the sporting venues, become branded products.[29] Once an Olympic host city has been branded in this way, it needs protection from non-sponsors that attempt to engage in ambush marketing strategies. These protections take many forms of both *lex Olympica* and Olympic law. The former is found in the requirements of Rule 50(1) of the Olympic Charter, which requires that all Olympic venues are 'clean' and free from any sponsorship and advertising, and Rule 40, which restricts athletes' ability to exploit their personal income streams. The latter is seen by the raft of legislation that is required to be enacted by hosts to restrict street trading, the unauthorised resale of event tickets, and, most importantly, ambush marketing.[30]

The remainder of this chapter examines the tensions created by the operation of Rule 40. We begin by defining its scope, purpose, and purview before examining its impact on Olympic athletes. This will expose the tensions between the IOC needing to maximise its commercial revenues to enable the celebration of the Olympic Games, whilst restricting the ability of the competing athletes to do the same for themselves, and between *lex Olympica* and national and EU law. This is a very specific example of *lex Olympica* in action.

The genesis and scope of the restrictions on athlete earnings

The modern Olympic Games are underpinned by the notion that sport should be practised for its own sake and not for reward. The IOC's ongoing refusal to pay athletes for their participation in the Olympic Games is born from its original insistence that all Olympians must be amateurs who receive neither financial nor political reward for their accomplishments. The introduction of the TOP Programme alongside allowing professional athletes to be invited to compete in the Olympic Games in the mid-1980s set the IOC and the athletes on an almost inevitable collision course about the fairness of income generation and its distribution, creating an explicit tension between athletes and the IOC. This has been exacerbated by the introduction of Rule 40 into the Olympic Charter in 1991, the aim of which was to protect the IOC's exclusive arrangements with the TOP Programme and the commercial value of being a member of this restricted group of sponsors. At the same time, it ensured that the brands that had provided Olympians with the financial and technical support to enable them to perform at the Games were excluded from associating with their athletes during what is often the highest profile time of their careers.

The prohibition on professionalism was extreme from the outset. Not only were professional athletes banned from competing; so were those earning a living from sport, such as physical education teachers, and those who received broken time payments as compensation for the loss of earnings suffered whilst travelling to and competing at the Games. The restriction that only amateurs could compete at the Olympics is found in Principle 1 of the first iteration of the Fundamental Principles and articulated in the 1924 edition of the Charter.[31] By 1949, the Fundamental Principles contain three specific mentions of amateurism: Principle 1, that the Olympic Games will assemble amateurs of all nations in fair and equal competition under conditions that are to be as perfect as possible; Principle 7, that only amateurs are eligible to compete; and Principle 8, that any financial surplus must be used for the promotion of the Olympic Movement or the development of amateur sport.[32] Rule 38 of the 1949 version of the Charter defines an amateur as:

> [O]ne who participates and always has participated in sport solely for pleasure and for the physical, mental or social benefits he derives therefrom, and to whom participation in sport is nothing more than recreation without material gain of any kind direct or indirect and in accordance with the rules of the International Federation concerned.

The absolute prohibition on payments found in Rule 26 was gradually relaxed and by 1962 allowed broken time payments and expenses to be paid to athletes whilst they were competing at the Olympics.[33] There were further explanations and relaxations to Rule 26 in 1972;[34] however, the prohibition continued to apply to athletes 'who are interested in sport for financial reasons alone.'[35] These developments were based on broader shifts in status and patterns in sport more generally. As Seltman states:

> From 1972 onwards, the institution was constantly adapted to reflect the realities of a commercialized sporting world, a new moral compass based on equity and democracy, and the power structures and partisan interests so dominant in the Olympic Movement.[36]

In this commercialised emerging landscape, and following a series of presentations by athletes to the XIth Olympic Congress in Baden-Baden, Germany, in 1981,[37] changes were eventually made to the Olympic Charter in 1985 that allowed the ISFs a wide discretion to determine the eligibility rules for the sports under their control. However, the bye-laws to Rule 26 still prohibited the participation of professional athletes in the Olympic Games.[38]

It was not until the 1991 version of the Olympic Charter that Rule 26 was finally removed and new eligibility criteria introduced in Rule 45.[39] This delegated responsibility for eligibility to the relevant ISF, subject only to approval by the IOC Executive Board. The only restrictions on earnings were found in bye-laws 4 and 5. Rule 45 bye-law 4 introduces the progenitor of Rule 40 and states that 'No competitor who participates in the Olympic Games may allow his person, name, picture or sports performances to be used for advertising purposes during the Olympic Games.' Bye-law 5 confirms that participation in the Olympic Games shall not be conditional on any financial consideration. Since then, these conditions have evolved into Rule 40 and restrict an athlete's ability to advertise for, or recognise the contribution of, their personal sponsors, unless of course these were also official sponsors of the IOC and/or of the specific edition of the Games in question.

Allowing professional athletes to compete, whilst restricting their ability to maximise their income from participation in the Olympics, created new tensions between the IOC and athletes. Principle 1 of the Fundamental Principles of Olympism states that Olympism seeks to create a way of life based on social responsibility and respect for universal fundamental ethical principles. Principle 4 states that the practice of sport is a human right and that participation in sport should be without discrimination of any kind, with mutual understanding, solidarity, and fair play. Further, Rule 2(11) of the Olympic Charter states that part of the IOC's mission is to oppose any commercial abuse of sport and athletes, with Rule 2(13) requiring the IOC to encourage and support the development of sport for all.

The operationalising of these Rules in the context of the Fundamental Principles of Olympism creates a tension between the promotion of a socially responsible, non-discriminatory mutuality of understanding of athletes' needs to generate a living income and their commercial exploitation for the financial benefit of the IOC. From a practical perspective, the Rule 40 restrictions make it more difficult for athletes from all backgrounds to exercise their human right to practise sport, to train and compete to the highest standards that enable them to compete in the Olympic Games. By restricting their ability to generate income, many prospective Olympians will be unable to fulfil their potential, arguably creating an indirectly discriminatory and socially irresponsible environment that excludes the participation of athletes from many countries and many sports.

Rule 40 and NOC guidance on advertising pre-2019

Since the introduction of the restrictions on athletes' earning power in 1991, the subsequent changes to what became Rule 40 have been driven by a combination of technological developments, particularly the growth in social media,[40] and athletes' collective activism. The enforcement of Rule 40 began in earnest at London 2012, where the use of social media was a game changer in terms of marketing and sponsorship. In response to the rigorous enforcement of Rule 40, athletes began to challenge its application by using #wedemandchange in their social media posts.[41] Despite a series of relaxations to Rule 40 post-London 2012, the IOC continued to protect its own revenue streams by preventing athletes from being paid to compete at the Olympics and restricting their advertising and sponsorship activities with non-Olympic sponsors during the Olympic blackout period.

The official purpose and policy justifications for Rule 40, as stated by the IOC, are '[to] preserve the unique nature of the Olympic Games by preventing over-commercialization,' and further, 'to allow the focus to remain on athletes,' whilst protecting the Olympics' source of funding, essentially the revenues generated by the official Olympic sponsors.[42] The practical function of Rule 40 is to protect the exclusive rights of official Olympic sponsors, including the members of the TOP Programme, to use all commercial property rights of the Olympic Games and to ensure that the IOC retains as close to absolute control of the Olympic spaces as is possible.

Although there were no changes to the wording of Rule 40 before the 2019 version of the Olympic Charter, the IOC began to relax its application by issuing guidance to athletes in advance of Rio 2016.[43] This saw a move away from the absolute prohibitions that were in place at London 2012 to a position where NOCs were expected to put in place a pre-approval, or waiver process, enabling a limited number of social media posts and non-Olympic sponsor endorsements to be permissible. This was of benefit to 'celebrity athletes' who were able to appear in ongoing 'generic' advertising campaigns throughout the Olympic Games.[44] This enabled athletes who were already engaged in advertising campaigns that began at a time determined by their NOC (usually between three and six months) before the Opening Ceremony to continue to appear in those ongoing campaigns, as long as it did not reference the Olympics and their participation in it. For those not engaged in such campaigns at the cut-off point, or not securing the necessary approval of their NOC, then they remained prohibited from having their name, image, and likeness used by a non-sponsor during the Games blackout period, which for Rio 2016 was from 27 July until 24 August 2016 (nine days prior to the Opening Ceremony until three days after the Closing Ceremony of the Rio 2016 Olympic Games). Despite these relaxations, for less well-known athletes or those not guaranteed to make the Olympic team, there was no practical change to the absolute prohibition. The problem for this group of athletes was that at the time of the deadline for seeking permission from their NOC, they had not yet qualified for the team. This left them still unable to engage with their personal sponsors on social media at the time of their greatest media exposure, making it virtually impossible to exploit commercially their participation in and successes at the Olympic Games.

Further detail was provided for PyeongChang 2018,[45] including a list of inadmissible practices and an expanded list of words that could not be used in adverts or social media posts. Inadmissible practices included the following:

- Any use of the Olympic properties or any NOC-related symbol including any expression creating a risk of confusion with these properties.
- Any express or implied written and/or visual allusion to the Olympic Games.
- Any use of an athlete's image taken during the Olympic Games and posted in combination with a non-sponsor's name or branding.
- Any reference to an athlete's participation in the Olympics, or to their performances at the current or any previous editions of the Games.
- Any use of the 'Olympic listed terms or expressions' (or anything closely resembling them) alongside the athlete's name or image, including: Olympic; Olympics; Olympic Games; Olympiad; Olympiads; and the Olympic motto 'Citius – Altius – Fortius' and any translation of the Olympic motto.
- Depending upon context, use of the following words was also restricted: 2018; PyeongChang; Gold; Silver; Bronze; Medal; Effort; Performance; Challenge; Winter; Games; Sponsors; Victory; and Olympian.

Thus, it was becoming increasingly apparent that the operation of Rule 40 was inconsistent with the commercial interests of professional athletes, and the IOC was faced with the first genuine threat to its sporting autonomy from Europe.

Challenging Rule 40: The increasing leverage of athletes

Over the past century, elite sport has undergone a fundamental shift from amateurism to professionalism. During this period, the IOC has become a hugely commercially successful multinational non-profit organisation funded entirely by broadcasting and licensing deals. The IOC's average annual revenues currently exceed $1.4 billion and although it states that 90% of its income is invested in the Olympic Games and athlete development, only 0.5% of its total spending goes directly to athletes, in the form of university athletic scholarships.[46] It is this disparity of income distribution that has resulted in the tension between the IOC's protectionism towards its own commercial revenue streams and the restrictions that it imposes on athletes to prevent them from profiting from their association with the Olympics during what for many will be one of the most lucrative times of their careers.

Despite being essential to the existence of a sport, athletes' economic and employment rights have been hard-won and often only grudgingly accepted by clubs, governing bodies, and competition and event organisers. The driving force behind these changes has been what Schwab has termed 'collective activism,'[47] which has enabled athletes to create associations, unionise, and/or engage in collective bargaining. This collective activism was instrumental to the Professional Footballers' Association's successful challenges to the maximum wage and retain and transfer systems that operated in English football into the 1950s and 1960s[48] and was central to Athleten Deutschland's ability to support the challenge to Rule 40. The creation of global unions such as the World Players Association, Global Athlete, and FIFPRO, has provided platforms for athletes around the world and across sports to challenge the restrictions placed on their commercial, employment, and human rights. Supported by a growing institutional activism, as epitomised by the work of bodies such as the Sport and Rights Alliance and the Centre for Sport and Human Rights, athletes are now much better placed to change the value systems of global sport.

London 2012 was a watershed moment for the Olympics as it was the first at which social media played a key part in both fans' and athletes' engagement with the Games. Of particular importance to the athletes was the additional guidance provided on the application of Rule 40 to social media posts. Its effect was to prohibit any social media engagement with, or reference to, non-Olympic sponsors, on threat of disqualification of the athlete from their event and expulsion from the Games. The strictness of these restrictions, in particular on athletes whose sponsors had enabled them to train, pay their expenses, and ultimately qualify for the Olympics, was an online backlash using the hashtag #wedemandchange.[49] The athletes' argument was that preventing them from engaging with their sponsors on social media restricted their ability to both generate income and maintain or develop their relationships with the sponsors who were integral to getting them to the Games.[50] In her review of the application of Rule 40 to social media posts at London 2012, Ormond notes with some prescience that 'In the age of social media, specifically, the increased use of Twitter, the time to amend Rule 40 is now, before it undoubtedly generates even more controversy.'[51] Having made clear her view on the impact of social media, she concluded that 'if Rule 40 is not amended to better serve athletes' interests, Rule 40 could eventually backfire on the IOC.'[52] As Bradish et al. summarised:

> Athletes should not have to pay to compete in the Olympics ... The athletes should be compensated for the opportunity cost of spending the prime years of their athletic careers training to compete in the Olympic Games. It is not as if the Olympics are unprofitable. If the Olympic organizations are unwilling or unable to compensate its athletes, it falls to the players to stand together for their rights and beliefs. If the IOC is truly against the commercial abuse of athletes, it will find a way to pay its athletes back. If not, it will be up to the athletes themselves.[53]

The organisation, or unionisation, of athletes has resulted in bodies that are more effective in challenging sports bodies' rules that have a negative impact on their economic, employment, and human rights. The result is that Olympic athletes, as collective actors, now constitute a severe challenge to the stability of the governance system of Olympic sports that has the potential to cause, and to a certain extent is already causing, substantial change to the defining institutions of the Olympic Movement.[54]

Despite the iterative development of Rule 40, the restrictions imposed on athletes became increasingly untenable, individually and collectively, and direct challenges began to be made. As McKelvey et al. observed:

> Brooks Running ran a stealth marketing campaign using Rule40.com tweets "to spotlight how Rule 40 unfairly penalizes athletes who are not famous."[55] Likewise, women's athletic leisure brand Oiselle's CEO was particularly vocal, alleging that even the relaxed Rule 40 for Rio 2016 did not give Olympic athletes enough flexibility to maintain a noticeable marketing presence by their personal sponsors during the Games period.[56]

The rationale behind the claims of unfairness from both the athletes and their sponsors was, and remains, that athletes' personal sponsors have invested heavily in them and enabled them to qualify for the Olympics, yet are restricted under Rule 40 from being able to advertise their sponsorship of the athlete during the peak Games period.[57] Meanwhile, the IOC and the members of the TOP Programme, which have not provided any support to the athlete throughout the qualifying period, are able to capitalise on the unpaid work of the athletes for their own commercial benefit, bluntly illustrating the tension between the athletes and the IOC, whilst illustrating further the need for a rebalancing of their relationship.

The conditions were ripe, therefore, for a challenge to be brought to relieve the tension between the IOC and the athletes to enable them to earn a living from their participation in the Olympic Games. The last significant obstacle that athletes faced before bringing a challenge to the legality of Rule 40 was that, in general, the IOC had been treated as though it was either immune from suit or that legal actions brought against it were not justiciable before national courts.

In the USA, challenges based on breaches of the Constitution of the United States and state law have failed against the United States Olympic Committee (USOC) because '[the] USOC is not a governmental actor to whom the Fifth Amendment applies'[58] and against the IOC because courts should be 'wary of applying a state statute to alter the content of the Olympic Games' as the event is 'organized and conducted under the terms of an international agreement – the Olympic Charter.'[59] In other words, any remedy should be sought directly from the IOC, not litigated before national or state courts. Similarly, it was held in Canada that the Canadian Charter of Rights and Freedoms did not apply to a challenge brought against the Vancouver Organising Committee for the 2010 Olympic and Paralympic Winter Games as this was a private body that was not carrying out policies or programmes on behalf of the government and over which the government did not exercise routine or regular control. [60] As Duval has noted, 'such self-restraint in embarking on a review of the [Olympic Charter] ("an international agreement") gives a lot of weight to the practical (if not formal) recognition of the autonomy and functional sovereignty of the Olympic regime.'[61] Further, challenges to advertising restrictions imposed by the USOC at the US Olympic Trials failed as there was an implied antitrust immunity for the USOC as otherwise, antitrust law would unduly interfere with the operation of the Amateur Sports Act 1978, which defines the mission of the USOC.[62]

Thus, in the leading cases prior to 2019 where the key Olympic stakeholders, including the IOC and local organising committees, were the defendant, an informal immunity from suit ensured that *lex Olympica* could only be challenged formally before the Court of Arbitration for Sport (CAS). As Rule 40 continued to be interpreted and enforced strictly, any challenge would need to prove both that cases brought against the IOC and any relevant NOC and/ or local organising committee were justiciable before national courts and then that the Rule 40 restrictions were unlawful.

The Deutscher Olympischer Sportbund case

The origins of the German challenge to the legality of Rule 40 began with the creation of Athleten Deutschland as a separate entity from the German NOC, the Deutscher Olympischer Sportbund (DOSB). Athleten Deutschland was established to promote more effectively the rights, concerns, and voice of German Olympic athletes. Its support for the action brought against the DOSB and the IOC by the Bundesverband der Sportartikel-Industrie (BSI), the Federal Association of the German Sports Goods Industry, proved crucial to the defeat of the Olympic bodies.

In 2017, the BSI submitted a complaint to the Bundeskartellamt (BKA), the German Federal Cartel Office, alleging that the advertising restrictions imposed on athletes and their personal sponsors by Rule 40 were incompatible with section 19(1) of the Act against Restraints of Competition and Articles 101 and 102 of the Treaty on the Functioning of the European Union (TFEU). The BSI's argument was simple: the DOSB and IOC were abusing their dominant position over the marketing arrangements for the Olympic Games by preventing both their members and the affected athletes from running marketing campaigns during the blackout period by the restrictions contained in Rule 40. The complaint was endorsed by Athleten Deutschland and, as part of its investigation, the BKA consulted with the athletes about the effects and impact of Rule 40 on them. At the time, German athletes were prevented from using a range of specific words, including Games, gold, silver, and bronze, and from using any photographs from the current, or previous, editions of the Olympic Games. Whilst the complaint was ongoing, the DOSB further relaxed its guidance and the BKA undertook market analyses during PyeongChang 2018 to assess the impact of the restrictions on the athletes and their personal sponsors.

In response to the BSI's claims, the IOC and DOSB claimed that Rule 40 was essential as it enabled the NOCs and the IOC itself to maximise their own income generation, again demonstrating the tension that existed in terms of their relationship with the athletes. The NOCs required these protections so that they could promote Olympism and send teams to the Olympic Games, whilst the IOC redistributed its income to NOCs, ISFs, local organising committees, and athletes through the Olympic Solidarity fund.[63] They claimed that any further relaxation of the DOSB's guidelines would endanger the Olympic Solidarity funding mechanisms and the organisation of a truly global Games with the widest possible participation.

The BKA made a number of preliminary findings. First, that the IOC and the DOSB were in a dominant position in the global market for the organisation and marketing of the Olympic Games. Secondly, that the restrictions contained in Rule 40 and the DOSB's accompanying guidance were an abuse of that dominant position. Thirdly, that the organisation and marketing of the Games were integral parts of a single product market, not separate markets. Fourthly, that existing protections in trademark, copyright, and under German national law, specifically the Act on the Protection of the Olympic Emblem and Olympic Names, were sufficient to enable the DOSB and IOC to generate the income needed to fund their activities. Fifthly, that there was no proof that any of the redistributed income went to the affected athletes.

The BKA found that the application of the then current iteration of Rule 40 on athletes and sponsors in Germany was a restriction of competition and that both the DOSB and the IOC were abusing their dominant position by means of a disproportionate response to the protection of their own income streams contrary to section 19(1) of the Act against Restraints of Competition and Article 102 of the TFEU. The BKA held that Rule 40 and its interpretation and application by the DOSB in its own guidance meant that the advertising restrictions on athletes and their personal sponsors were an abuse of the dominant position of the DOSB and IOC. In particular, account was taken of the fact that the athletes as the performers in the Olympic Games do not benefit directly from the very high advertising revenues generated by the official Olympic sponsors.

The authority of the BKA and its standing on matters of interpretation of competition law mean that it is extremely likely that any subsequent legal action would come to similar conclusions on the legality of Rule 40 throughout the European Union. Although resolved by means of commitments, meaning that the findings lack the level of detail and status as a legal precedent that would be expected of an opinion of the European Court of Justice or European Commission, the BKA's preliminary assessment establishes that restricting the commercial behaviour of athletes and their personal, non-Olympic sponsors is an abuse of a dominant position. The binding commitments provided by the IOC and DOSB to the BKA were to relax even further the Rule 40 restrictions.

The initial impact of the BKA case was limited; the IOC and DOSB agreed to relax the guidance on Rule 40, but that this should only apply to the DOSB and to the athletes chosen to represent Germany at the Olympic Games. As it became apparent that this would lead to further legal challenges, both from EU Member States where a similar outcome could be almost guaranteed and elsewhere on the basis that all athletes should be given the same opportunities to generate income, the IOC relented in 2019 and rewrote Rule 40(3):

> Competitors, team officials and other team personnel who participate in the Olympic Games may allow their person, name, picture or sports performances to be used for advertising purposes during the Olympic Games in accordance with the principles determined by the IOC Executive Board.

This change can be read in several ways. First, as a pragmatic response by the IOC to avoid further challenges to the primacy of *lex Olympica* and litigation of the Olympic Charter. Secondly, as a delegation of responsibility to the NOCs, which may be better placed to ensure the compliance of Rule 40 with the national laws of the countries in which they are based. Thirdly, as an abrogation of responsibility for the operationalisation of its Rules and their impact on athletes. Although many NOCs, particularly those from the Global North, took advantage of the opportunity to relax their Rule 40 guidance, many others have not. This is likely to cause confusion, and further litigation, in the future as there is the potential for multiple interpretations of Rule 40, including from each of the 204 NOCs, from the IOC, from CAS, and from the courts and competition authorities before which any future challenges are commenced.

The DOSB case is a landmark decision that has resulted in the rewriting of *lex Olympica* in two ways: first, Rule 40 was revised to grant the NOCs wide-ranging discretion over how they would regulate the personal sponsorship arrangements of their own athletes. Secondly, it resulted in changes to the athletes' agreements with their NOCs.[64] Rule 40 in its original form was highly restrictive and a clear and obvious restriction on athletes' earnings potential. The successful challenge by the BSI and Athleten Deutschland resulted in the IOC revising its legal norm in this area and stepping away from regulating this area by delegating responsibility to the NOCs. The tension between protecting the IOC's income streams at the expense of restricting athletes' earnings was reduced significantly by the collective action of the athletes forcing a change in the *lex Olympica*. However, the revised Rule 40 has the potential to create further tensions as there is now no set paradigm by which all NOCs must operate, leaving some athletes able to exploit more freely their commercial rights, whilst others cannot, leading to further distortion of an already uneven playing field.

The contemporary landscape: Tokyo 2020 and beyond

The revised Rule 40 was used for the first time at Tokyo 2020 and was operational for a shorter blackout period running from the date of the Opening Ceremony, 13 July 2021, until two days after the Closing Ceremony, 10 August 2021. Interpretative guidance was issued by the IOC,[65] alongside detailed online advice from the IOC Athletes Commission, which was reissued in the same form for Beijing 2022.[66] The IOC's guidance was based on five key principles.[67] First, to protect their own income streams, advertising by Olympic Partners was permitted in line with their agreements with the IOC and securing any necessary consents from the athlete. Their advertising can use the Olympic Properties and in-venue images of athletes. Secondly, advertising by non-Olympic Partners must notify the relevant NOC prior to the commencement of the campaign by 15 May 2021, must be generic, and must not use any Olympic Properties or prohibited words or phrases. Thirdly, personal sponsor advertising must be generic, in that it must not suggest a link between the athlete and the Olympics (such as advertising a car or a watch), and the campaign must have started 90 days before the start of the blackout period. Fourthly, congratulatory messaging is only allowed by Olympic Partners during the blackout period. Fifthly, athletes are permitted only one thank you message per personal sponsor, but must not suggest that their performance was enhanced by the personal sponsor's support, and must not endorse the personal sponsor's products or services.

It was accepted by President Bach that there could be no one-size-fits-all solution because of the differing attitudes of individual NOCs towards their own and their athletes' commercial activities and the different legal frameworks within which they operate.[68] However, by delegating responsibility for the creation and enforcement of Rule 40 guidance to the NOCs, there can be no consistency of approach to its operation globally. Athletes from different countries, but with the same personal sponsor, may be subject to very different restrictions depending on the permissiveness of their own NOC's approach.[69] This in turn could lead to the possibility of confusion about who can do what and where, and to inadvertent breaches of Rule 40.

Each NOC is responsible for implementing these principles in its own territory. Some NOCs have provided very detailed guidance that is significantly more athlete-centric than the IOC's principles, presumably on the basis that in these territories the law would require a more permissive approach. At the other extreme, where a NOC has issued no further guidance, athletes will be bound by the IOC's interpretation of Rule 40. The diversity of approaches used by NOCs to interpret their delegated powers under the revised Rule 40 framework has been tracked by McKelvey et al.[70] At one extreme, the DOSB has the most permissive regime. German athletes' sponsors do not need to seek approval of advertising campaigns, can start them during the blackout period, and can send unlimited congratulatory messages. German athletes have much fewer restrictions on what they can post on social media, including words, phrases, and hashtags that would be prohibited in other countries. The more moderate approaches of the Australian and Canadian Olympic Committees generally follow the IOC guidance with some relaxations: the Australian athletes are allowed to thank their personal sponsors once for every time that they compete; the personal sponsors of Canadian athletes can post one congratulatory message and share one athlete thank you message during the course of the Games, providing that the Olympic Properties are not used. At the other extreme, the USOPC adopted a novel approach that, whilst allowing some relaxations to the IOC's principles, imposed an additional layer of regulation on athletes and their personal sponsors. To be able to take advantage of these relaxations, Team USA athletes were required to register their personal sponsors with the USOPC and each registered personal sponsor was required to sign a Personal Sponsorship Commitment Agreement (PSCA). The PSCA enables the USOPC to sue an athlete's personal sponsor for breach of contract should they infringe the USOPC's Rule 40 guidelines or engage in any other ambush marketing activities.

The resultant lack of consistency of approach amongst NOCs leaves significant scope for further challenges to the operation of Rule 40 around the world, dependent upon the precise nature of the restrictions imposed by each NOC, its legal personality, and the national and transnational laws under which it operates. McKelvey and Grady identify a number of legal problems with the USOPC approach, including that the contract is lacking effective consideration from the USPOC, that the terms are too vague to enforce, that there are no means of establishing when a breach has occurred, and that no appropriate dispute resolution mechanism is identified. There are likely to be similar problems of enforceability and accountability in the guidance provided by other NOCs. As McKelvey and Grady conclude:

> While the creation of the PSC process is a clever mechanism for controlling ambush marketing through contract law, the contract as presented to personal sponsors arguably places them in an untenable situation of not only putting their sponsored athletes at risk by violating the contract, but also agreeing to curtail marketing activities that they otherwise would have the legal right to do.[71]

European concepts of competition law have, therefore, reshaped how *lex Olympica* operates, though other jurisdictions may have further impact on its future development. Rule 40 has moved from a position of universal prohibition to one that is more permissive and that has the potential to be of significant benefit to athletes, provided that they are representing a NOC that supports athletes being able to generate income from their participation in the Olympics. The changes, forced on the IOC and only grudgingly accepted as necessary and appropriate by them, may ultimately increase tensions with the athletes rather than relieve them.

Conclusion

The importance of the DOSB case cannot be overestimated. First, it has demonstrated that the Olympic Charter is justiciable before national courts and does not have immunity from suit. *Lex Olympica* must comply with national and EU law unless the deviation from those laws can be justified as being necessary and proportionate. As is the case with *lex sportiva*, *lex Olympica* has only conditional autonomy from the operation of the law.[72] Sport has often fallen short when trying to explain the necessity and proportionality of its restrictive rules, and to date, the IOC has proved to be no exception. In any future litigation, the IOC will need to demonstrate that any restrictions imposed on athletes are necessary and proportionate to promote the Fundamental Principles of Olympism, and promote fairness and openness in sporting competitions, and cooperation between the various bodies responsible for the organisation of sports.[73] If such restrictions were developed relationally, in conjunction with the athletes through engagement with appropriately independent Athlete Commissions and/or global athlete unions, then there is a greater chance that these will be upheld as lawful. The unilateral imposition of such restrictions simply paves the way for future legal challenges.

Although the German challenge to Rule 40 was successful, comparatively few NOCs, predominantly from the Global North, have taken advantage of the opportunity to relax their restrictions. From a practical perspective, the IOC has delegated responsibility for operationalising Rule 40 to the NOCs. In theory, this could lead to different interpretations of the legality of any remaining restrictions by each of the 204 NOCs, the IOC, CAS, and each of the national and transnational courts and competition authorities that could have jurisdiction over a dispute. The DOSB case has relieved some of the tension between the IOC and the athletes and rebalanced its relationship with German and EU law. However, new tensions are likely to emerge that could lead to further litigation in the future. It would have been easier to work with the athletes and negotiate relationally to a mutually beneficial compromise, rather than resolving the dispute by legal means.

The majority of athletes will continue to need to generate their own income to be able to compete at major championships, including the Olympics.

By denying them the commercial opportunities provided by participation in the Games, the IOC is in effect self-harming and acting in a manner that is contrary to the Fundamental Principles of Olympism by preventing the widest possible range of athletes from being given the best opportunity to compete at the Olympics. Whilst the IOC is able to 'commercially abuse' the Games for its own profit, athletes cannot do the same to earn a living without falling foul of either Rule 40 or the Olympic laws required of hosts to protect against ambush marketing. As has been seen, the law can be used to relieve the tensions and rebalance the relationship between the IOC and the athletes. Further, it is likely to be resorted to again in the future, especially as the IOC is seeking to include Olympic qualifying events within the scope of its regulatory influence.[74] As this could reduce even further the opportunity for athletes to benefit directly from their personal sponsorships, a more cooperative, relational way of negotiating a compromise looks increasingly important.

There is, therefore, a clear need to reappraise and rebalance the relationship between the IOC and the athletes and to ensure that the enforcement of the *lex Olympica* against athletes is done so in accordance with both the Fundamental Principles of Olympism and national laws. As is proposed in Chapter 5, Relational Contract Theory would provide a framework within which the current tensions could be relieved; neither side wants to alienate or antagonise the other unnecessarily, otherwise there will be no Games. The need to maintain effective working relationships between the IOC and its key stakeholders should drive these changes, not the IOC's desire to prevent others from profiting in its thematic space.

This example shows a common pattern of response from the IOC. Initially, it simply states its legal norms, the *lex Olympica*, and expects that everybody will do as they are told, enabling it to exploit its own commercial agendas, whilst restricting the opportunities of athletes to act in a similar way. The formal challenge to Rule 40 has rebalanced the relationship between the IOC and the athletes, but has also seen the IOC simply absolve itself of responsibility for the enforcement of the relaxed restrictions, leaving the potential for confusion and inadvertent breach, instead of a uniform approach across the Olympic Movement. Having examined the tensions at the heart of the income generation framework that governs the athletes, the IOC and the NOCs, we now turn to the issue of the controls placed on the athletes' freedom of expression and social activism.

Notes

1 Rule 40(4) of the Olympic Charter (2021).
2 There is a voluminous literature on this topic. See, for example, Zimbalist, A (2003) 'Sport as Business' 19(4) *Oxford Review of Economic Policy* 503–511, and Sodeman, S and Dolles, H (2013) *Handbook of Research on Sport and Business* (Edward Elgar, Cheltenham).

3 Slack, T (ed) (2003) *The Commercialisation of Sport* (Taylor & Francis Group, London).
4 Westerbeek, H and Smith, A (2003) *Sport Business in the Global Marketplace* (Springer, New York), Gratton, C and Kokolakakis, T (2018) 'Sport in the Global Marketplace' in Hassan, D (Ed) *Managing Sport Business* (2nd ed, Routledge London), ch 2.
5 Pound, R (2021) 'Olympic Values: Sponsorship, Values and Integrity in Sport Creating a Paradigm Shift' in Chatziefstathiou, D, Garcia, B and Seguin, B (eds) *Routledge Handbook of the Olympic and Paralympic Games* (Routledge, Oxford), ch 7.
6 Coors, C (2015) 'Are Sports Image Rights Assets? A Legal, Economic and Tax Perspective' 15(1–2) *International Sports Law Journal* 64–68.
7 Greenfield, S and Osborn, G (2001) *Regulating Football* (Pluto Press, London).
8 James, M and Osborn, G (2011) 'London 2012 and the Impact of the UK's Olympic and Paralympic Legislation: Protecting Commerce or Preserving Culture?' 74(3) *Modern Law Review*, 410–429.
9 Meenaghan, J (1991) 'The Role of Sponsorship in the Marketing Communications Mix' 10 *International Journal of Advertising* 35–47. For an overview of the definitions of both sponsorship and sports sponsorship, see Nufer, G (2013) *Ambush Marketing in Sports* (Routledge, Oxford), ch 2.
10 Llewellyn, M, and Gleaves, J (2016) *The Rise and Fall of Olympic Amateurism* (University of Illinois Press, Chicago). For a shorter overview, see Wagg, S (2012) 'Tilting at Windmills? Olympic Politics and the Spectre of Amateurism' in Lenskyj, H and Wagg, S (eds) *The Palgrave Handbook of Olympic Studies* (Palgrave Macmillan, Basingstoke), ch 20.
11 *Gold Medal, LLC. v USA Track & Field*, 899 F.3d 712 (9th Cir. 2018). Although unsuccessful in the US courts, similar arguments were ultimately successful in the German litigation on the interpretation and application of Rule 40 of the Olympic Charter, discussed later in this chapter.
12 Pound, R (2021) 'Olympic Values: Sponsorship, Values and Integrity in Sport Creating a Paradigm Shift' in Chatziefstathiou, D, Garcia, B and Seguin, B (eds) *Routledge Handbook of the Olympic and Paralympic Games* (Routledge, Oxford), ch 7.
13 Whannel, G (2012) 'The Rings and the Box: Television Spectacle and the Olympics' in Lenskyj, H and Wagg, S (eds) *The Palgrave Handbook of Olympic Studies* (Palgrave Macmillan, Basingstoke), ch 16.
14 Neirotti, L (2020) 'Olympic Broadcast Rights' in Chatziefstathiou, D, Garcia, B and Seguin, B (eds) *Routledge Handbook of the Olympic and Paralympic Games* (Routledge, Oxford), ch 10.
15 IOC (2022), *Olympic Marketing Fact File 2022 Edition*, p. 19, available at: https://stillmed.olympics.com/media/Documents/International-Olympic-Committee/IOC-Marketing-And-Broadcasting/IOC-Marketing-Fact-File.pdf (last accessed 05/01/2023).
16 Pound, R (2021) 'Olympic Values: Sponsorship, Values and Integrity in Sport Creating a Paradigm Shift' in Chatziefstathiou, D, Garcia, B and Seguin, B (Eds) *Routledge Handbook of the Olympic and Paralympic Games* (Routledge, Oxford), ch 7.
17 Ibid, p 82.
18 Bradish, C, Koehler, R and Bailey, A (2019) *Olympic Commercialization and Player Compensation: A Review of Olympic Financial Reports*, available at: https://mcusercontent.com/84af2d82b4ff06bd42452dbf8/files/39f1fd06-9ec8-4ca3-85b1-a9d392aefaad/2020.04.22_Olympic_Commercialization_and_Player_Compensation_FINAL.pdf, at 4 (last accessed 17/02/2023).

19 Johnson, P (2008) 'Look Out!' It's an Ambush' 7(2–3) *International Sports Law Review* 24–29 and Grady, J, McKelvey, S and Bernthal, M (2010) 'From Beijing 2008 to London 2012: Examining Event-Specific Olympic Legislation vis-à-vis the Rights and Interests of Stakeholders 3(2) *Journal of Sponsorship* 144–156.

20 James, M and Osborn, G (2018) 'Pliant Bodies: Generic Event Laws and the Normalisation of the Exceptional' 12(1) *The Australian and New Zealand Sports Law Journal* 77–96.

21 James, M and Osborn, G (2016) 'The Olympics, Transnational Law and Legal Transplants: The International Olympic Committee, Ambush Marketing and Ticket Touting' 36(1) *Legal Studies* 93–110; and Grady, J (2020) 'Legal Aspects of the Olympics and Ambush Marketing' in Chatziefstathiou, D, Garcia, B and Seguin, B (eds) *Routledge Handbook of the Olympic and Paralympic Games* (Routledge, Oxford), p 133.

22 Nufer, G, (2013) *Ambush Marketing in Sports*, (Routledge, Oxford), at 58 and also Grady, J (2020) 'Legal Aspects of the Olympics and Ambush Marketing' in Chatziefstathiou, D, Garcia, B and Seguin, B (eds) *Routledge Handbook of the Olympic and Paralympic Games* (Routledge, Oxford), ch 12.

23 Meenaghan, T, (1994) 'Point of View: Ambush Marketing: Immoral or Imaginative Practice?' 34(5) *Journal of Advertising Research* 77–89, at 79.

24 See Abeza, G (2021) 'The Olympic Games and ambush marketing via social media' available at: https://olympicanalysis.org/section-1/the-olympic-games-and-ambush-marketing-via-social-media/ and IOC (2019) *Tokyo Brand Protection Guidelines*, available at: https://gtimg.tokyo2020.org/image/upload/production/wcrldxxeeicwze8v4y4i.pdf (both last accessed 17/02/2023).

25 Ellis, D, Scassa, T and Seguin, B (2011), 'Framing Ambush Marketing as a Legal Issue: An Olympic Perspective' 14(3) *Sport Management Review* 297–308.

26 For more on these and other classic examples of ambush marketing at the Olympic Games, see Epstein, A (2017) 'The Ambush at Rio' 16 *The John Marshall Review of Intellectual Property Law* 350–380.

27 Burton, N and Chadwick, S (2018) 'Ambush Marketing is Dead, Long Live Ambush Marketing' 58(3) *Journal of Advertising Research* 282–296, at 289.

28 See Stein, A (2023) 'Ambush Marketing: The Italian Zalando Case' 45(3) *European Intellectual Property Review* 176–179 for a rare case of a successful prosecution of ambush marketing under Italian law.

29 Osborn, G and Smith, A (2015) 'Olympic Brandscapes: London 2012 and the Seeping Commercialisation of Public Space' in Poynter, G, Viehoff, V and Li, Y (eds) *The London Olympics and Urban Development: The Mega-Event City* (Routledge, London), 139–153.

30 James, M and Osborn, G (2011) 'London 2012 and the Impact of the UK's Olympic and Paralympic Legislation: Protecting Commerce or Preserving Culture?' 74(3) *Modern Law Review*, 410–429.

31 IOC (1924) *Olympic Charter*, available at: https://library.olympics.com/Default/doc/SYRACUSE/42078/statuts-du-comite-international-olympique-reglements-et-protocole-de-la-celebration-des-olympiades-m (last accessed 11/01/2023).

32 IOC (1949) *Olympic Charter*, available at: https://library.olympics.com/Default/doc/SYRACUSE/70124/olympic-rules-international-olympic-committee (last accessed 11/01/2023).

33 IOC (1962) *Olympic Charter – Eligibility Rules of the International Olympic Committee*, available at: https://library.olympics.com/Default/doc/SYRACUSE/21014/regles-du-comite-international-olympique-sur-les-conditions-d-admission-aux-jeux-olympiques-eligibil (last accessed 22/02/2023). See also, Andrews, R (2018) 'Push to Allow Professional Athletes Took Hold in 1968 Olympic Games'

Global Sport Matters 15 October, available at: https://globalsportmatters.
com/1968-mexico-city-olympics/2018/10/15/professional-athletes-1968-olympic-
games/ (last accessed 06/01/2023).
34 IOC (1072) *Olympic Charter*, available at: https://library.olympics.com/Default/
doc/SYRACUSE/54477/the-olympic-games-rules-and-regulations-international-
olympic-committee (last accessed 21/02/2023).
35 Schwab, B (2018) '"Celebrate Humanity": Reconciling Sport and Human Rights
Through Athlete Activism' 28(2) *Journal of Legal Aspects of Sport* 170–207, at
186 et seq.
36 Seltman, M (2021), 'Disrupting Institutional Reproduction? How Olympic Athletes Challenge the Stability of the Olympic Movement' 18(1) *Sport und Gesellschaft* 9–37, at 18.
37 Oliver, B (2021), '"We said things we weren't allowed to say" – when athletes
challenged the IOC and were finally given a voice' *Inside The Games*, 26 September, available at: https://www.insidethegames.biz/articles/1113448/big-read-
michelle-ford-athlete-voice (last accessed 06/01/2023).
38 IOC (1985) *Olympic Charter*, available at: https://library.olympics.com/Default/
doc/SYRACUSE/172334/olympic-charter-1985-international-olympic-committee
(last accessed 21/02/2023).
39 IOC (1991) *Olympic Charter*, available at: https://library.olympics.com/Default/
doc/SYRACUSE/172354/olympic-charter-in-force-as-from-16th-june-1991-inter-
national-olympic-committee (last accessed 21/02/2023).
40 Abeza, G (2020) 'The Evolving #Rule40 of the Olympic Charter: Balancing the
Interest of Sponsors vs Athletes' in Chatziefstathiou, D, Garcia, B and Seguin,
B (eds) *Routledge Handbook of the Olympic and Paralympic Games* (Routledge,
Oxford), ch 13.
41 Ormond, M (2014) '#WeDemandChange: Amending International Olympic Committee Rule 40 for the Modern Olympic Games' 5 *Journal of Law, Technology &
the Internet* 179–200.
42 IOC (2021) *Commercial Opportunities for Participants During the Rescheduled
Olympic Games Tokyo 2020 (in 2021)*, available at: https://olympics.com/athlete365/
app/uploads/2021/02/2021-02-03-Tokyo-2020-Commercial-Opportunities-
for-Athletes-Key-Principles-FINAL.pdf (last accessed 16/02/2023), at 2.
43 McKelvey, S, Grady, J and Moorman, A (2021) 'Ambush Marketing and Rule 40
for Tokyo 2020: A Shifting Landscape for Olympic Athletes and Their Sponsors'
31 *Journal of Legal Aspects of Sport* 94–122, at 99, and Abeza, G (2020) 'The
Evolving #Rule40 of the Olympic Charter: Balancing the Interest of Sponsors vs
Athletes' in Chatziefstathiou, D, Garcia, B and Seguin, B (eds) *Routledge Handbook of the Olympic and Paralympic Games* (Routledge, Oxford), at 141. The
guidance is available at: https://stillmed.olympic.org/Documents/Athletes_Infor-
mation/Rule_40-Rio_2016-QA_for_Athletes.pdf (last accessed 06/01/2023).
44 Finlay, C J (2018) 'The Right to Profitable Speech: Olympians, Sponsorship, and
Social Media Discourse' 6(6) *Communication and Sport* 655–679.
45 IOC (2018) *Rule 40 Guidelines, XXIII Olympic Winter Games PyeongChang 2018*,
available at: https://www.insidethegames.biz/media/file/85618/FINAL%20-%20
Rule%2040%20Guidelines%202-%20ENG.pdf (last accessed 21/02/2023).
46 Bradish, C, Koehler, R and Bailey, A (2019) *Olympic Commercialization and
Player Compensation: A Review of Olympic Financial Reports*, available at:
https://mcusercontent.com/84af2d82b4ff06bd42452dbf8/files/39f1fd06-9ec8-
4ca3-85b1-a9d392aefaad/2020.04.22_Olympic_Commercialization_and_Player_
Compensation_FINAL.pdf, at 4 (last accessed 17/02/2023).
47 Schwab, B (2018) '"Celebrate Humanity": Reconciling Sport and Human Rights
Through Athlete Activism' 28(2) *Journal of Legal Aspects of Sport* 170–207, at
186 et seq.

48 See here *Eastham v Newcastle United FC Ltd* [1964] Ch 413, and Greenfield, S and Osborn, G (2001) *Regulating Football* (Pluto Press, London).

49 Ormond, M (2014) '#WeDemandChange: Amending International Olympic Committee Rule 40 for the Modern Olympic Games' 5 *Journal of Law, Technology & the Internet* 179–200.

50 Abeza, G (2020) 'The Evolving #Rule40 of the Olympic Charter: Balancing the Interest of Sponsors vs Athletes' in Chatziefstathiou, D, Garcia, B and Seguin, B (eds) *Routledge Handbook of the Olympic and Paralympic Games* (Routledge, Oxford), at 142.

51 Ormond, M (2014) '#WeDemandChange: Amending International Olympic Committee Rule 40 for the Modern Olympic Games' 5 *Journal of Law, Technology & the Internet* 179–200, at 181.

52 Ibid, at 184. On digital ambush marketing at London 2012, more generally see Chanavat, N and Desbordes, M (2014) 'Towards the Regulation and Restriction of Ambush Marketing? The First Truly Social and Digital Mega Sports Event: Olympic Games, London 2012' 15(3) *International Journal of Sports Marketing & Sponsorship* 2–11.

53 Bradish, C, Koehler, R and Bailey, A (2019) *Olympic Commercialization and Player Compensation: A Review of Olympic Financial Reports*, available at: https://mcusercontent.com/84af2d82b4ff06bd42452dbf8/files/39f1fd06-9ec8-4ca3-85b1-a9d392aefaad/2020.04.22_Olympic_Commercialization_and_Player_Compensation_FINAL.pdf at p17 (last accessed 17/02/2023).

54 Seltman, M (2021) 'Disrupting Institutional Reproduction? How Olympic Athletes Challenge the Stability of the Olympic Movement' 18(1) *Sport und Gesellschaft* 9–37, at 11.

55 Quoting Li, S. (2016) 'Olympics bans most brands from saying 'Olympics' or 'Rio,' even on Twitter. Snark ensues' *Los Angeles Times*, 11 August, available at: https://www.latimes.com/business/la-fi-olympics-rule-40-20160802-snap-story. html (last accessed 06/01/2023).

56 McKelvey, S, Grady, J and Moorman, A (2021) 'Ambush Marketing and Rule 40 for Tokyo 2020: A Shifting Landscape for Olympic Athletes and Their Sponsors' 31 *Journal of Legal Aspects of Sport* 94–122, at 100.

57 Belson, K (2012) 'Olympians Take to Twitter to Protest Endorsement Rule' *New York Times*, July 30. Available at: https://www.nytimes.com/2012/07/31/sports/olympics/athletes-at-olympics-protest-sponsorship-rule-on-twitter.html (last accessed 06/01/2023).

58 *San Francisco Arts & Athletics, Inc. v United States Olympic* Committee 483 U.S. 522 (1987), at 523.

59 *Martin v International Olympic Committee* 740 F.2d 670 (9th Cir. 1984), at 677.

60 *Sagen v Vancouver Organizing Comm. for the 2010 Olympic and Paralympic Winter Games*, 2009 BCSC 942 (Can BC).

61 Duval, A, (2018), 'The Olympic Charter: A Transnational Constitution Without a State?' 45(S1) *Journal of Law and Society* S245–269, at S263.

62 *Gold Medal, LLC. v USA Track & Field*, 899 F.3d 712 (9th Cir. 2018) and further, McKelvey, S, Grady, J and Moorman, A, (2021) 'Ambush Marketing and Rule 40 for Tokyo 2020: A Shifting Landscape for Olympic Athletes and Their Sponsors' 31 *Journal of Legal Aspects of Sport* 94–122, at 102.

63 IOC (2022), *Olympic Marketing Fact File 2022 Edition*, available at: https://stillmed.olympics.com/media/Documents/International-Olympic-Committee/IOC-Marketing-And-Broadcasting/IOC-Marketing-Fact-File.pdf (last accessed 05/01/2023).

64 For more detail on this development, see McKelvey, S, Grady, J and Moorman, A, (2021) 'Ambush Marketing and Rule 40 for Tokyo 2020: A Shifting Landscape for Olympic Athletes and Their Sponsors.' 31 *Journal of Legal Aspects of Sport* 94–122.

65 IOC (2021) *Commercial Opportunities for Participants During the Rescheduled Olympic Games Tokyo 2020 (in 2021)*, available at: https://olympics.com/athlete365/app/uploads/2021/02/2021-02-03-Tokyo-2020-Commercial-Opportunities-for-Athletes-Key-Principles-FINAL.pdf (last accessed 16/02/2023).

66 IOC/Athlete 365 information hub on Rule 40 available at: https://olympics.com/athlete365/rule-40/ (last accessed 17/02/2023).

67 IOC (2021) *Commercial Opportunities for Participants During the Rescheduled Olympic Games Tokyo 2020 (in 2021)*, available at: https://olympics.com/athlete365/app/uploads/2021/02/2021-02-03-Tokyo-2020-Commercial-Opportunities-for-Athletes-Key-Principles-FINAL.pdf (last accessed 16/02/2023).

68 AP (2019) 'IOC resists change to Olympic rule limiting athlete sponsors' *USA Today*, 14 April, available at: https://eu.usatoday.com/story/sports/olympics/2019/04/14/ioc-resists-change-to-olympic-rule-limiting-athlete-sponsors/39344465/ (last accessed 17/02/2023).

69 The IOC's own advice acknowledges this specifically, 'As a result, the implementation of these Principles by NOCs may vary.' IOC (2021) *Commercial Opportunities for Participants During the Rescheduled Olympic Games Tokyo 2020 (in 2021)*, available at: https://olympics.com/athlete365/app/uploads/2021/02/2021-02-03-Tokyo-2020-Commercial-Opportunities-for-Athletes-Key-Principles-FINAL.pdf (last accessed 16/02/2023), at 2.

70 McKelvey, S, Grady, J and Moorman, A (2021) 'Ambush Marketing and Rule 40 for Tokyo 2020: A Shifting Landscape for Olympic Athletes and Their Sponsors' 31 *Journal of Legal Aspects of Sport* 94–122.

71 McKelvey, s, Grady, J and Moorman, A (2021) 'Ambush Marketing and Rule 40 for Tokyo 2020: A Shifting Landscape for Olympic Athletes and Their Sponsors' 31 *Journal of Legal Aspects of Sport* 94–122, at 118.

72 Weatherill, S (2012) 'Is There Such a Thing as EU Sports Law' in Siekmann, R and Soek, J (eds), *Lex Sportiva: What is Sports Law?* (TMC Asser Press, The Hague), at 305.

73 Article 165 Treaty of the Treaty on the Functioning of the European Union.

74 Owen, D (2022) 'The devil in the detail of IOC-driven qualifying event reforms' *Inside the Games*, 8 November, available at: https://www.insidethegames.biz/articles/1130171/david-blog-reforms#.Y2uB2_jjvZM.twitter (last accessed 17/02/2023).

4 Freedom of Expression and the Olympics

Introduction

In this chapter, the focus moves on to one of the most contested areas of athlete regulation: freedom of expression. The scope and effect of the restrictions imposed exemplify the tension that exists between the International Olympic Committee's (IOC's) own attitude towards human rights and the actual human rights of the athletes that the IOC seeks to circumscribe. The same analytical approach used in Chapter 3, to examine the commercial restrictions imposed on athletes under Rule 40 of the Olympic Charter (Rule 40), is used here to analyse the evolution of the restriction on athletes' freedom of expression, through an analysis of Rule 50(2) of the Olympic Charter (Rule 50). At the Olympic Games, Rule 50 prohibits any kind of 'demonstration or political, religious or racial propaganda' in Olympic venues and the Olympic Village. Although there is yet to be a challenge to the legality of Rule 50 that is analogous to how the German Olympic athletes and their personal sponsors successfully challenged the restrictions in Rule 40, legal action of some kind is almost inevitable should the IOC decide to enforce Rule 50 against athlete activists. This highlights another key tension between how the IOC claims to act and how it actually acts in practice. The IOC claims to promote and protect human rights through the development of its Strategic Framework on Human Rights,[1] whilst imposing restrictions on athletes' ability to protest and exercise their own right to freedom of expression.[2] Once again, using athlete activism as an example, it can be demonstrated how the law can be used to rebalance the relationship between the IOC, *lex Olympica*, and the athletes in a more co-operative, mutually beneficial, and relational way. Before looking specifically at Rule 50, its evolution is situated in the broader context of the often uneasy relationship between politics and sport more generally.

Political theorists have noted that, notwithstanding the importance of sport in commercial terms, and in many ways its centrality to our global political cultures, remarkably little attention has been paid to the area by political scientists.[3] Whilst this lacuna may seem surprising, that is not to say that the political and the sporting have neither coincided nor clashed.[4] The role of

DOI: 10.4324/9780429323355-4

sport in confronting and ultimately precipitating the demise of apartheid in South Africa is a particularly cogent case in point.[5] From an Olympic-consumer perspective, the terms and conditions of Olympic tickets for spectators limit what can be taken into specific venues and facilities.[6] For example, at London 2012, the Terms and Conditions of Tickets contain the stipulation in clause 19.2.3 that various items were prohibited from being brought into stadia including the '[flags] of countries not participating in the Games.'[7] From a political perspective, it was designed to prevent protests over contested states, such as Taiwan flying its national flag inside the stadiums, and the use of non-state flags, such as the Japanese sunburst flag.[8] The issue of flags returned to prominence following the Court of Arbitration for Sport's (CAS's) decision to prohibit the Russian delegation from competing as Russia at Tokyo 2020 and Beijing 2022,[9] providing a further example of the intersections between sport and politics. Cha notes that the 'mutual neglect' of sport and politics in terms of academic treatment diminished after Moscow 1980[10] and has become even more pronounced when we consider *participation* rather than *consumption*. As Malik has noted, all athletic endeavour is in fact grounded in social context.[11] So sport and politics are intertwined and away from the Olympics, 2016 witnessed the beginning of a new wave of athlete activism that grew out of support for San Francisco 49ers' quarterback Colin Kaepernick 'taking the knee' during the American National Anthem, to protest against social injustice and police brutality in the United States of America. Coupled with the widespread support for the Black Lives Matter movement following the killing of George Floyd by Minneapolis police, and related anti-discrimination protests, athlete activism has become more widespread and of higher profile in recent years.

It is within this context that this chapter focuses on the evolution of athlete activism, and the restrictions imposed on activist athletes, at the Olympic Games. As with Chapter 3 and its treatment of Rule 40, this chapter examines how athletes' freedom of expression is defined and policed, primarily via Rule 50. The analysis illustrates the operation of and challenges to the *lex Olympica* hegemony and in particular the tension created by the IOC's claims to protect, respect, and provide remedies for breaches of human rights with its explicit restrictions on athletes' freedom of expression, for which no specific grievance mechanism is provided. We begin by considering the history of athlete activism at the Olympic Games and the evolution of Rule 50.

Olympians and activism

Athlete activism has produced some of the most iconic moments in modern Olympic history. Although controversial at the time, their importance to the Olympic Movement, and sport and society more generally, demonstrates clearly that these high-profile protests can be catalysts for change.

Cottrell and Nelson have identified several characteristics that help to explain why the Olympic Games are such an attractive platform for activism:[12] that the Olympics are accessible and high-profile, with almost all states invited to attend, ensuring that any protest is likely to attract significant media attention; that activists can expect to forge new alliances with like-minded others as a result of their activism; and that, as the Olympics are attributed special symbolic meaning by athletes, consumers, and nations, there is a resultant widening of political opportunity. Kluch has reviewed the evolution of the definition(s) of athlete activism, providing a wider context in which the Rule 50 protests can be analysed, defining athlete activism as:

[Athletes'] and other sport peoples' use of their involvement in sport as a platform to promote social justice, the goal of which Bell ... describes as the "full and equitable participation of people from all social identity groups in a society that is mutually shaped to meet their needs."[13]

Although focusing on American college athletes, the definitions are arguably of universal application and describe the behaviours identified as athlete activism at the Olympics. A further gloss can be added to this from Cooper et al., whose typology of sports activism defines 'symbolic activism' as the 'calculated and strategic protests aimed at increasing awareness of social injustice in an attempt to promote positive social change.'[14] Here, the focus is on individual, symbolic activism engaged in by athletes, or small groups of like-minded athletes, and its relationship with Rule 50.

Whilst there had been isolated incidents of athlete protests at previous Olympic Games,[15] Mexico 1968 marks the starting point of the modern, mediated athlete activist. Three incidents in particular caught the mood of the athletes at a time of political tensions around the world. First, and most famously, was the Black Power salute of US athletes John Carlos and Tommie Smith, supported by Australian silver medallist Peter Norman wearing an Olympic Human Rights Project badge.[16] Smith and Carlos were sent home by the IOC, utilising its powers under Rule 23 of the Olympic Charter, and ostracised for many years by the United States Olympic and Paralympic Committee (USOPC) and the wider Olympic Movement. Secondly, Czech gymnast Vera Čáslavská looked down and away from the winners' flags whilst the Russian national anthem was played during the medal ceremony for the (controversially awarded) joint gold medallists. Thirdly, while accepting their medals for the 400 m, Lee Evans, Larry James, and Ron Freeman wore Black Panther style berets and all three raised their fists, as Smith and Carlos had. However, they lowered them and removed their berets when the national anthem was played and the American flags were raised.[17] This compromise ensured that no further action was taken against them by the IOC.

Each of these protests against social and political injustice are now considered to be iconic moments of athlete activism. Only with the benefit of hindsight are these activists celebrated for their bravery: Carlos and Smith were inducted into the USPOC Hall of Fame in 2019;[18] Norman was posthumously awarded the Olympic Order of Merit by the Australian Olympic Committee in 2018;[19] Čáslavská became President of the Czech Olympic Committee and, in 1995, a member of the IOC;[20] and Evans, a founding member of the Olympic Project for Human Rights, was inducted to the USOPC Hall of Fame in 1989.[21]

A key recent development has been the significant impact of the Black Lives Matter movement. This became of more immediate importance to the IOC when, at the 2019 Pan-American Games, US hammer thrower Gwenn Berry and fencer Race Imboden, respectively, raised a fist and took the knee on their medal podiums.[22] The high-profile nature of these demonstrations, and the athletes' status as potential participants at Tokyo 2020, caused Thomas Bach to state that 'The Olympic Games ... are not, and must never be, a platform to advance political or any other potentially divisive ends.'[23] In January 2020, the first guidance on the operation of Rule 50 was published by the IOC Athletes' Commission.[24] This stated unequivocally that all protests and/or demonstrations taking place during an event, in the Olympic Village, or during the opening, closing and medal ceremonies were prohibited. In particular, 'gestures of a political nature,' including specifically hand gestures and kneeling, were identified as being in breach of Rule 50. Any proven breach could lead to the disqualification of the athlete and the removal of their Olympic accreditation. Although this guidance was later modified, it reinforces the IOC's approach to athlete activism: *it is not welcome at the Olympic Games.*

More widespread, but generally accepted manifestations of politics and religion can be seen when athletes cross or prostrate themselves, usually before or at the end of a performance, or when they salute or place their hands on their hearts during medal ceremonies or whilst anthems are playing. The lack of justification for the differential application of Rule 50 is a key problem with the transparency of its interpretation. Although there are no reported uses of Rule 50, or any of its previous iterations, against any of the athletes mentioned above, its use was threatened at both Sochi 2014 and Tokyo 2020. The guidance on the interpretation and potential application of Rule 50 provides the context in which the restrictions of athletes' freedom of speech can be analysed.

The genesis and scope of the restrictions on athlete protest

Despite the many claims that sport should keep out of politics, and vice versa, and that the IOC and Olympic Games should remain politically neutral, the two remain intimately intertwined.[25] In an attempt to prevent a repetition of the highly politicised Berlin 1936 Olympics, the Olympic Charter was amended in 1956 to specifically prohibit political demonstrations by stating that nobody was to profit commercially or politically from their participation in the Games.[26] This prohibition was at first not part of the main body of the Charter, but constituted 'General Information' about the Games in the section, 'The Olympic Games are Amateur.'[27] Anyone breaching this prohibition could be punished under what was then Rule 23 of the Olympic Charter, which stated that, as the Supreme Authority, the IOC was the final arbiter on all questions concerning the Olympic Games and the Olympic Movement. It was this power that enabled IOC President Avery Brundage to impose the expulsion of Tommie Smith and John Carlos from Mexico 1968.

The aim of these prohibitions was to preserve the political neutrality of the Olympics, which are supposed to be a sporting competition between individual athletes and teams, not nations. This focus on the competitors, as opposed to their national teams, even extended to a refusal to produce an official medal table, as this would encourage competition between nations:[28]

All things considered, the IOC perceives and projects itself as a neutral entity, which is further confirmed through its governing rules and even its seat in Switzerland further reflects this self-perception.[29]

This self-perception, or perhaps self-deception, fails to appreciate how politics continually influences and has an impact onthe Olympic Movement in general, and the Olympic Games in particular. The IOC's observer status at the United Nations, the promotion of the Olympic Truce, the recognition of National Olympic Committees as representatives to and of nation states, the failure to recognise some NOCs because of objections from other states (for example, Taiwan competes as Chinese Taipei), the use of national flags and anthems, and opening ceremonies that promote the host nation and its iconography can all be seen as integral parts of the politicisation of sport in general, and the Olympics in particular, through sports nationalism.[30] However much the IOC may try to create a clean political environment, to match its requirements of a clean commercial environment in Rules 40 and 50(1) of the Olympic Charter, 'politics are structurally embedded within the Games due to the array of actors representing a variety of interests that are involved in its planning and execution,' and as a result 'the Games can never truly take place within an impenetrable bubble that is somehow separated from the societal context in which it takes place.'[31]

Despite keeping politics out of sport being an impossible task, the IOC's response to the protests at the 1968 Games was to begin the process of updating and reinforcing the Olympic Charter to attempt to do just this. The 1971 edition of the Olympic Charter gave greater prominence to the prohibition by placing it in a new section of the Instructions headed, 'The Olympic Games are not for Profit,' though without changing the wording. Following further protests by US athletes Vincent Matthews and Wayne Collett at Munich 1972,[32] the prohibition was finally included in the main body of the Olympic

Charter as part of the wide-ranging Rule 55 under the subheading 'Advertising, propaganda' so that: 'Every kind of demonstration or propaganda, whether political, religious or racial, in the Olympic areas is forbidden.' In 1978, Rule 55 was broken down into separate issues, resulting in the prohibition on athlete activism being elevated to the status of a Rule of the Olympic Charter in its own right:

57 Propaganda and advertising

Every kind of demonstration or propaganda, whether political, religious or racial, is forbidden in the Olympic areas.

Finally, in 2011, we see the current version of Rule 50 for the first time:

50 Advertising, Demonstrations, Propaganda

No kind of demonstration or political, religious or racial propaganda is permitted in any Olympic sites, venues or other areas.

Throughout this period, there was no specific justification for the prevention of athlete activism provided by the IOC, except for the general statement that politics should be kept out of sport. Further, there were no prescribed means of investigating and prosecuting a suspected breach of Rule 50 or its predecessors, providing the IOC with an incredibly wide-ranging discretion to determine when it considered that an athlete had overstepped the mark.

The contemporary landscape: Rule 50 and the 2021 Guidance

The Fundamental Principles of Olympism can be read as either a corporate mission statement or, in more legalistic terms, as the interpretative norms that shape the meaning of the Rules that follow.[33] According to four of these seven Fundamental Principles, Olympism is based on: social responsibility and respect for universal fundamental ethical principles (Principle 1); the preservation of human dignity (Principle 2); and that the rights and freedoms contained in the Charter must be secured without discrimination of any kind, including specifically on the grounds of religion, political, or other opinion (Principle 6). Further, Olympism considers the practice of sport to be a human right that must be carried out with mutual understanding, a spirit of friendship, solidarity, and fair play (Principle 4). The only mention of political neutrality is in Principle 5, which requires that sports organisations, not athletes, should be free from outside political interference when adhering to the principles of good governance. This is reinforced by Rule 2(6) of the Olympic Charter, which states that the mission of the IOC requires it to act against any form of discrimination affecting the Olympic Movement, and Rule 2(11), which requires the IOC to oppose any political or commercial abuse of sport and athletes.

Where the Fundamental Principles of Olympism and the mission of the IOC seek to promote social responsibility, human dignity, anti-discrimination, and freedom of religious and political thought, Rule 50(2) seeks to limit the extent to which athletes can exercise these rights. The current version of Rule 50(2) and relevant bye-laws read as follows:

50 Advertising, demonstrations, propaganda

2. No kind of demonstration or political, religious or racial propaganda is permitted in any Olympic sites, venues or other areas.

Bye-law to Rule 50

1. No form of publicity or propaganda, commercial or otherwise, may appear on persons, on sportswear, accessories or, more generally, on any article of clothing or equipment whatsoever worn or used by all competitors, team officials, other team personnel and all other participants in the Olympic Games, except for the identification … of the manufacturer of the article or equipment concerned, provided that such identification shall not be marked conspicuously for advertising purposes.

The IOC Executive Board shall adopt guidelines that provide further details on the implementation of this principle.

Any violation of this Bye-law 1 and the guidelines adopted hereunder may result in disqualification of the person or delegation concerned, or withdrawal of the accreditation of the person or delegation concerned, without prejudice to further measures and sanctions which may be pronounced by the IOC Executive Board or Session.

The numbers worn by competitors may not display publicity of any kind and must bear the Olympic emblem of the [Organising Committee of the Olympic Games].[34]

The wording of Rule 50 provides for an absolute prohibition of demonstrations or the dissemination of propaganda at the Olympic Games. Despite this prohibition, it has not been relied on as a means of punishing athletes' behaviour by the IOC, only to threaten punishment if the behaviour continues. At Sochi 2014, a number of athletes were warned that if their behaviour was repeated, this could constitute a breach of Rule 50. This included the silver medal winning Ukrainian cross-country ski team covering their medals with their hands whilst the Russian national anthem was playing for the gold medallists, an overtly political statement, protesting the then recent annexation of

Crimea by Russian forces. At the other extreme, members of the Norwegian cross-country skiing team wore black armbands to commemorate the death on the eve of the Games of one of their team's brothers and training partners.[35] This act of remembrance was also considered to be unlawful propaganda, despite the wearing of a commemorative armband being neither a political, religious nor racial statement.[36] This more lenient approach of warning, rather than a formal finding that a breach of Rule 50 had occurred, was continued at Rio 2016, when Ethiopian athlete Feyisa Lilesa crossed his hands, to represent being shackled, in a protest against the oppression of the Oromo people.[37]

The Olympic Charter in general, and Rule 50 in particular, is reinforced by the Olympic Athletes' Declaration.[38] Point 11 of the Declaration on Athletes' Rights 'aspires to promote the ability and opportunity of athletes to … free expression.' In counterpoint, the Athletes' Responsibilities encourage athletes to 'refrain from political demonstration in competitions, competition venues and ceremonies' at point five and to 'inform themselves and be aware of their responsibilities' at point eight. Taken together, the position under the Charter and the related documents is that freedom of expression is an aspiration to be encouraged, but imposes very specific limitations on that freedom to ensure what the IOC considers to be the imperative of political neutrality. The explosion of athlete activism from 2019 onwards alerted the IOC to the possibility that protests were likely to occur at Tokyo 2020. In his New Year Message of January 2020, IOC President Thomas Bach acknowledged this possibility and reiterated that all protests were prohibited and that guidance on the application of Rule 50 would be forthcoming:

> The Olympic Games … are not, and must never be, a platform to advance political or any other potentially divisive ends. We stand firmly against the growing politicisation of sport because only in this way can we accomplish our mission to unite the world in peaceful competition … Athletes have an essential role to play in respecting this political neutrality [and] the field of play and Games ceremonies should not become an arena for political statements or any kind of protests. Respecting one's fellow athletes also means respecting their unique Olympic moment and not distracting from it with one's own political views.[39]

The final version of the Guidance, produced in conjunction with the IOC Athletes' Commission and published on 2 July 2021, provides a level of specificity not previously seen.[40] It explains not only the purpose of Rule 50, but when and how athletes can exercise their freedom of expression, should they wish to do so. The document begins by explaining that the focus of the Olympic Games is on athletes' performance and international unity and that this neutrality must be separated from 'political, religious or any other type of interference.' This is because athletes' 'moment of glory,' whether during a competition or at official ceremonies, must be respected and protected.

This means that the more neutral 'expressions,' as opposed to the 'protests and demonstrations' referred to in the original version, are not permitted during the opening, closing and medal ceremonies, during competition, and in the Olympic Village. In other words, Rule 50 is there to prevent demonstrations and protests (expressions) from occurring at the time and place where they would be most effective.

The Guidance also states when and where athletes are able to exercise their freedom of expression. These include the mixed zones, the International Broadcasting Centre and the Main Media Centre, during press conferences in the venue or in the Main Media Centre, during interviews, at team meetings, in traditional or digital media, and through social media channels. In a surprising concession to responses to the consultation with Athletes' Commissions around the world,[41] it was also stated that athletes can express their views:

> On the field of play prior to the start of the competition (i.e. after leaving the "call room" (or similar area) or during the introduction of the individual athlete or team) provided that the expression (for example, gesture) is:

> i consistent with the Fundamental Principles of Olympism;
> ii not targeted, directly or indirectly, against people, countries, organisations and/or their dignity;
> iii not disruptive (by way of example only, the following expressions are considered disruptive: expressions during another athlete's or team's national anthem and/or introduction, as this may interfere with such other athlete's or team's concentration on and/or preparation for the competition; physical interference with the introduction of another athlete or team or the protocol itself (for example by unfurling a flag, a banner etc.); causing (or assuming the risk of causing) physical harm to persons or property, etc.); and
> iv not prohibited or otherwise limited by the rules of the relevant National Olympic Committee and/or the competition regulations of the relevant International Federation.[42]

This relaxation of the impact of Rule 50 allows athletes to take the knee prior to the start of their event, provided that the remaining conditions are also fulfilled. Further, when exercising their (limited) freedom of expression, athletes are expected to respect the relevant laws of the host nation, Olympic values, and their fellow athletes. Any behaviour that constitutes or signals discrimination, hatred, hostility, or the potential for violence on any basis whatsoever will continue to be a breach of Rule 50. This could be a particular problem in some host jurisdictions, where national laws restrict or prohibit protests or demonstrations either generally or when focused on specific topics.

One of the tensions we identify, between the rights and values defined as being integral to Olympism and the way that the IOC restricts the rights and values that it claims to be promoting, is clearly evident in the way that Rule 50 and its accompanying interpretative guidance conflicts with the Fundamental Principles of Olympism. This tension is exacerbated by the interpretation of Rule 50 and the accompanying guidance, and the way that these were applied at Tokyo 2020.

Rule 50: Interpretative issues and definitional problems

To be able to analyse the impact of Rule 50 on the acts of athlete activism that took place at Tokyo 2020, it is necessary to determine the nature and scope of the 'expressions' that it seeks to prohibit. First, there is no definition of what constitutes a 'demonstration' or 'propaganda' in the Charter, although it is clearly aimed at prohibiting 'protests,' in the widest meaning of the term, in specific Olympic venues and during specific events. The Guidance, which uses the more neutral term 'expression,' provides no further definition of what is to be prohibited, though the example of a 'gesture' is given as an example of the kind of 'expression' that could be problematic. This gives rise to an important distinction and the first potential area of confusion: all political, religious, and racial demonstrations and propaganda are prohibited, but freedom of expression is merely limited.

If 'demonstration' is given its widest meaning, it would include any politically, religious, and/or racially motivated gesture, action, or statement, rendering the Guidance nugatory. If given a narrower meaning, as appears to be envisaged by the Guidance, then it becomes necessary to be able to distinguish between 'demonstrations' that are overtly political, religious, and/ or racial and 'expressions' that promote general issues of social justice, anti-discrimination, and inclusion.

From a practical perspective, this requires an analysis of specific gestures, actions, and statements, and the intention behind why they were performed in the place, manner, and at the time they were performed, to determine whether they are prohibited 'demonstrations' or 'propaganda' that should be sanctioned under Rule 50, or an acceptable exercise of an athlete's freedom of expression, as promoted by the Athlete Declaration. Prior to Tokyo 2020, unacceptable gestures had included: raising a fist; taking the knee; wearing a black armband as a mark of bereavement; crossing one's arms at the finish line; waving an unofficial flag; looking away from the winner's flag during a medal ceremony; covering one's medal whilst the anthem of another country was playing; discarding one's medal and exiting the arena; and not taking the medal ceremony seriously enough. On the other hand, acceptable gestures have included: crossing oneself or genuflecting before, during, or after an event; saluting one's flag; and placing one's hand on one's heart during a medal ceremony or whilst the national anthem is being played. Each of these gestures, regardless of the category into which the IOC would prefer to place them, could be considered to be either an unacceptable political, religious, or racial demonstration or an acceptable expression of religion, nationality, or support for an issue of social justice and inclusion. This gives rise to a second unexplained difficulty with Rule 50 and its guidance: there is no explanation of, or attempt at justifying why, this wide range of gestures requires different treatment or outright prohibition.

The inconsistent approach to defining what is covered by the term 'expressions' is exacerbated by the inconsistent application of Rule 50, not only by the IOC, but also by the international sports federations and NOCs. In the months before Tokyo 2020, the President of World Athletics, Lord Coe, stated that there would be no punishments for athletes using gestures to support campaigns for social justice.[43] Similarly, FIFA and UEFA supported footballers taking the knee before games and those who wanted to wear rainbow laces and armbands in support of LGBTQ rights. Conversely, World Swimming took a more prohibitive stance than was provided for in the Guidance.[44] Swimmers in all disciplines were banned from making any demonstrations or expressions poolside, despite pre-event gestures being allowed under the IOC's Guidance. Further inconsistencies could be seen in the responses of the NOCs. Where most remained silent on how they would interpret and apply Rule 50, the USOPC stated that 'Prohibiting athletes to freely express their views during the Games, particularly those from historically underrepresented and minoritized groups, contributes to the dehumanization of athletes that is at odds with key Olympic and Paralympic values.'[45] A significant number of other NOCs stated that they would not punish their athletes should they decide to exercise their freedom of expression for similar purposes.

This in turn leads to the third major problem with Rule 50; that it leaves the IOC with an incredibly wide discretion when it comes to its interpretation. Under the Guidance, the IOC expects to delegate enforcement of Rule 50 to the NOCs in the first instance. The International Sports Federations (ISFs), as signatories to the Olympic Charter, would also have standing to apply it. If neither the athlete's NOC nor the relevant ISF considers a breach to have occurred, then the IOC retains the ability to investigate and apply Rule 50 against any athlete it still considers to be in breach. For example, when Team USA shot putter Raven Saunders crossed her hands in an 'X' to signify the intersection of where all those who are oppressed meet at the end of her medal ceremony,[46] the USOPC stated that as far as it was concerned, there was no breach of Rule 50. World Athletics were not asked to intervene, but it can be assumed on the basis of Lord Coe's previous statements that it too would have considered that there were no grounds for further investigation. Despite the USOPC's findings, the IOC continued to investigate Saunders until she returned home following the death of her mother, at which point the IOC suspended its proceedings. The different approaches of the many ISFs, NOCs, and the IOC also mean that there is a genuine risk of Rule 50 being applied inconsistently, unless a single, independent body investigates all potential infractions of Rule 50. This could cause particular problems if, for example, there was a mass protest at an opening, closing, or medal ceremony, where some NOCs and ISFs were prepared to impose a restrictive interpretation, whilst others were not.

Finally, it is possible for athlete activists to claim that their 'demonstrations' are not grounded in political, religious, or racial activism, and therefore are not in breach of Rule 50, because they are proactively supporting or promoting the Fundamental Principles of Olympism.[47] This approach was utilised specifically at Sochi 2014 by the Principle 6 campaign. Instead of criticising directly Russia's 'anti-gay' laws, athletes promoted LGBTQI+ rights by promoting the anti-discrimination agenda defined in Principle 6 of the Fundamental Principles, ultimately resulting in the addition of sexual orientation to the list of protected characteristics. Thus, an athlete could claim that their demonstration, propaganda, or expression was not politically motivated but supported:

- social responsibility and respect for universal fundamental ethical principles (Principle 1);
- promoting a peaceful society concerned with the preservation of human dignity (Principle 2); and
- anti-discrimination (Principle 6).

As the IOC claims that it operates in a politically neutral way, then by actively promoting the Fundamental Principles of Olympism, athletes are acting inherently apolitically when exercising their freedom of expression.[48] Again, however, this would require a clear distinction to be made between overtly political demonstrations and expressions in support of the types of causes championed by the Olympic Movement. Overall, the lack of clear definitions for the key behaviours leads to a Rule that is open to inconsistency in both its interpretation and application, resulting in unfairness to those athletes engaging in activism in and around the Olympic Games.

Tokyo Storm Warning: Rule 50 at Tokyo 2020

Despite the warnings from President Bach, the reiteration of Rule 50, and the interpretative Guidance produced by the Athletes' Commission, there were many and varied cases of demonstrations, propaganda, and/or expressions by activist athletes at Tokyo 2020.[49] Although some attracted the attention of the IOC, only one athlete was subsequently accused of breaching Rule 50 by his ISF, and in the majority of cases no action of any kind was taken. On the one hand, this could be seen as an enlightened approach by the IOC and/or the Tokyo Organising Committee, allowing the athletes their moment and leaving it to the media to determine whether or not the expression was about an issue worth covering. On the other, the IOC can be accused of failing to provide proactive leadership on the issues raised by the athletes, leaving everyone in a position of even less clarity on how and why Rule 50 will apply in the future. To determine whether a breach of Rule 50 has occurred, the IOC or its delegates must prove either that: an athlete had engaged in a demonstration or act of political, racial, or religious propaganda; or that the exercise of the athlete's freedom of expression was a breach of the Guidance. This latter investigation will include determining whether: the expression is consistent with the Fundamental Principles of Olympism; is not targeted, directly or indirectly, against people, countries, organisations and/or their dignity; is not disruptive of the event or ceremony; and is not illegal in the host nation.

Five cases provide exemplars of the inconsistency of approach to the application of Rule 50 at Tokyo 2020. In all but one of the cases, the problematic 'expressions' took the form of a gesture of some kind. The remaining case, and the only one that resulted in the formal punishment of the athlete, involved the withdrawal of an athlete on politico-religious grounds and for acting in a discriminatory manner. In this case, Algerian judoka, Fethi Nourine, was sent home and had his Olympic accreditation withdrawn by the Algerian Olympic Committee and was subsequently banned for 10 years by the International Judo Federation when he withdrew from his event because of the possibility of facing an Israeli athlete in the second round. His behaviour was found to breach the IJF's Code of Conduct and Rule 50.[50]

In each of the remaining four cases, the conduct of the athletes could be considered a *prima facie* breach of Rule 50 as it was a demonstration with an underlying political, racial, or religious undertone or was targeted at a specific individual. However, each was treated differently for reasons that are not always clear. First, Chinese gold medal cyclists Bao Shanju and Zhong Tianshi, who wore badges featuring the head of the country's former leader Mao Zedong during their medal ceremony.[51] This was considered by the IOC to be a political statement in breach of Rule 50. After receiving assurances from the Chinese Olympic Committee that the athletes concerned had been warned about their conduct and that there would be no repetition by other members of their delegation, the matter was closed.[52] Secondly, after the completion of her medal ceremony, American shot putter, Raven Saunders, crossed her hands in an 'X' to signify the intersection of where all those who are oppressed meet.[53] The IOC asked the USOPC to investigate whether her action constituted a breach of Rule 50; its conclusion was that there was no infringement and that her conduct was compliant with the USOPC's code of conduct and the IOC's Guidance.

Thirdly, no action was taken against the American fencing team when they wore pink face masks to show solidarity with the survivors of sexual violence and abuse. Although on the face of it a laudable exercise of their freedom of expression, the three members of the team wearing pink had not informed the fourth member of the team, Alan Hadzic, that they were going to do this, leaving him alone in wearing a black mask. Hadzic was, at the time, being investigated for three counts of sexual assault.[54] This demonstration was, arguably, in breach of the Guidance by being, at least indirectly, targeted at a specific individual; however, no action was taken by the IOC. Fourthly, German field hockey captain, Nike Lorenz, was granted permission by the IOC to wear a rainbow band on her sock to signify her support of LGBTQI+ rights.[55] As the IOC had given its permission, it must have considered that this was neither a demonstration, nor political propaganda, or that it was in support of the anti-discrimination message in Principle 6 of the Fundamental Principles of Olympism. However, no explanation was given for why this was allowed, nor what the process for acquiring permission was so that other athletes could act in a similar fashion. Finally, Team GB's women's footballers were the first to take advantage of the relaxations in the Guidance by taking the knee before their opening game against Chile.[56]

These examples demonstrate that only the most overt forms of political statement are likely to be considered to infringe Rule 50. However, only the actions of Team GB's footballers are definitively in compliance with the Guidance. The remaining actions, as well as others engaged in by athletes at Tokyo 2020, fall into a grey area where it is unclear whether a breach of Rule 50 has occurred. The lack of explanations for why the investigation of Saunders was dropped, how and why permission was granted to Lorenz, and why no action was taken against the American fencers leaves the interpretation and application of Rule 50 unclear and inconsistent. We now examine in more detail the tension between the IOC's claims that it is a protector of human rights and the restrictions on those human rights that it imposes on athletes, how those restrictions might be challenged, and how this tension might be ameliorated.

Challenging Rule 50: A different kind of tension

The tensions identified from the interpretation and application of Rule 50 at Tokyo 2020 are clear. On one level, the IOC's commitment to protecting, respecting, and remedying human rights can be contrasted with its determination to protect the political neutrality of the Olympic Games by restricting athletes' freedom of expression.[57] Further, having determined to implement the restrictions defined in Rule 50 and the Guidance, its application to the incidents that took place at Tokyo 2020 demonstrates a lack of transparency and an inconsistency of approach. The existence and application of Rule 50 tests the boundaries of *lex Olympica*, as Rule 40 did previously. It identifies the fractured nature of human rights protections in sport and the tensions between public pronouncements on human rights strategies and the failure to protect, respect, and, especially, provide remedies for their infringement. The position of many members of the Olympic Movement is exemplified by a statement from World Athletics that as it is not a public authority exercising state powers, but rather a private body exercising contractual powers, it is not subject to human rights instruments such as the Universal Declaration of Human Rights and the European Convention on Human Rights (ECHR).[58] For athletes seeking a remedy, questions remain over whether this should be provided by the IOC, as Supreme Authority of the Olympic Movement, the Ad Hoc Division of Court of Arbitration for Sport (CAS) at the Games where the expression was made, the CAS on appeal from a decision of the IOC, an ISF or NOC, the Swiss Federal Tribunal (SFT) on appeal from CAS, or the European Court of Human Rights (ECtHR) on appeal from the SFT. As both the IOC and CAS are located in Switzerland, which is a signatory of the ECHR, then actions against the Swiss state for its failure to protect the human rights of those affected either by organisations located there or by arbitral processes taking place there are most easily challenged by actions before the ECtHR.[59]

These tensions, contradictions, and an overarching lack of transparency mean that if an athlete is sanctioned for breaching Rule 50, a legal challenge is almost inevitable. More fundamentally, it questions whether, and to what extent, the IOC has a responsibility to respect international human rights instruments in its dealings with athletes. If an athlete is suspected of breaching Rule 50, there are two potential sources of punishment. First, the IOC and/or NOC can investigate and prosecute the breach, with the power to disqualify and/or remove the accreditation of the offending athlete indefinitely. Secondly, the athlete's ISF can impose sanctions, as happened with Algerian judoka Fethi Nourine.[60] Regardless of the route pursued, an appeal can be made to CAS against the findings of the IOC, the relevant NOC, and/or the sport's ISF.

If a punishment is imposed by either the IOC or an athlete's NOC or ISF, for a breach of Rule 50, a first appeal can be made to CAS, either its Ad Hoc Division sitting at the Games itself or the full tribunal in Lausanne under Rule 61 of the Olympic Charter. From here, there are limited opportunities of appeal to the SFT, and from there to the ECtHR.[61] This approach follows the same litigatory trail followed by Claudia Pechstein.[62]

In determining any appeal, CAS would need to interpret and apply Rule 50 to the relevant incident. In doing so, the panel must apply Swiss Law,[63] and according to its own jurisprudence, it will apply 'universal legal norms' in its determination of the dispute.[64] If CAS decides that restrictions on an athlete's freedom of expression fall within its jurisdiction, then it could decide on the merits of Rule 50, including whether it conforms with Article 10. Following *Pechstein*, as CAS is required to adhere to the requirements of Article 6(1) of the ECHR, then, by analogy, CAS could decide that all claims founded on breaches of the Convention are also within its jurisdiction.[65] This would enable it to determine whether the protection of political neutrality in sport is a legitimate aim for restricting athletes' freedom of expression. Alternatively, as Swiss law is the governing law of disputes involving the IOC, then the ECHR can be applied, or its values have to be taken into consideration when interpreting the grounds for appeal.[66]

Further, all state signatories to the ECHR are not only under a negative obligation to avoid infringing human rights themselves, but are also under a positive obligation to create an environment in which everyone is able to express their opinions and ideas without fear. In practice, this means that the state must act to protect athletes' freedom of expression against abuses by non-state actors.[67] This horizontal application of the ECHR ensures that where a Swiss-based organisation such as the IOC restricts Convention rights, it must act lawfully when doing so, or action can be taken by the affected athlete against Switzerland to terminate the abuse. Regardless of the route of appeal, the European Court of Human Rights will have ultimate jurisdiction over any challenge to the legality of Rule 50.

To determine the legality of a restriction on an athlete's freedom of expression under Article 10 ECHR, four criteria must be addressed: is Rule 50 an interference with the athlete's freedom of expression; is that interference prescribed by law; does the interference serve a legitimate aim; and is the interference necessary and proportionate in a democratic society?

Without good reasons for the restrictions, and despite the spatial and temporal limitations on its operation, by preventing the exercise of their freedom of expression, and in particular their ability to comment on political issues and matters of public importance and debate, there is a *prima facie* restriction on athletes' freedom of expression under Article 10 ECHR.

Although Rule 50 is spatially and temporally restricted in its operation, the lack of specificity of its definitions and transparency of its application runs the risk of it being found to be both insufficiently precise to be considered 'law' and, as such, unnecessary and disproportionate. Further, the inconsistent application of Rule 50 renders it almost impossible to determine in advance whether any act of athlete activism is permitted or prohibited. The absence of a legally robust justification for prohibiting athlete activism is compounded by the IOC's own lack of consistency when enforcing its stance on political neutrality. For example, at the insistence of the People's Republic of China, Taiwan is not recognised as an independent state, but is allowed to send athletes to the Olympics provided that they compete as Chinese Taipei, use the flag of the Chinese Taipei Olympic Committee, and do not play the Taiwanese national anthem.[68] Thus, the IOC is political in its actions, whilst limiting the politicisation of others, rendering the sporting neutrality argument inconsistent and unsystematic.[69]

The restrictions imposed on athletes' freedom of expression do not appear to be necessary for the purpose of protecting the IOC's sporting neutrality. As athletes provide increasingly nuanced justifications for their actions and base them on both generic causes, such as the need to improve social justice, and causes underpinned by the Fundamental Principles of Olympism, such as anti-discrimination and inclusion, they distance themselves from the overt politicking at which Rule 50 was originally directed. As the ability to exercise one's freedom of political expression is more important to the operation of a democratic society than the IOC's contested assertion that it is politically neutral, Rule 50 appears to be an unnecessary restriction on athletes' freedom of expression.

Further, the breadth and application of Rule 50 and the punishments imposed for its breach are not proportionate to its stated aim. Any restriction on freedom of expression must meet a pressing social need, be the least interference possible to meet the legitimate aim, and there must be relevant and sufficient reasons for the imposition of the restriction.[70] First, without an underpinning 'legitimate aim,' it is difficult to argue that there is a pressing social need for the restrictions imposed by Rule 50; it could be argued with equal force that there is a pressing social need for athlete activists to be able to use their profile and platform to help to challenge structural injustices and discrimination of all kinds. The unlimited range of potential punishments is also disproportionate; at Tokyo 2020, these ranged from the IOC ignoring or taking no action against a demonstration, to Nourine's 10-year ban. Without further explanation of why a punishment is being imposed, any sanction looks more like an unfettered exercise of the IOC's discretion to act as the Supreme Authority of the Olympic Movement.

In its current form, Rule 50 would likely be found to breach Article 10 of the ECHR. The justification for its existence, based on the political neutrality of sport, is too vague and inconsistently applied by the IOC itself. As can be seen from the approach undertaken at Tokyo 2020, the application of Rule 50 lacks consistency of rationale, making it difficult to justify either its legitimacy of purpose or inherent legality. Save for the most extreme and targeted of demonstrations or expressions, it will be difficult to show that there is a compelling social need for Rule 50 that is necessary in a democratic society.[71] If the Swiss state is unable to justify why the IOC's restrictions are legitimate, necessary, and proportionate, it could be found to have violated Article 10 by its failure to protect athletes from the effects of Rule 50. A finding that Rule 50 is unlawful would allow athletes greater scope to exercise their freedom of expression, provided that, as role models, they do so responsibly.[72] The IOC would have a narrow margin of appreciation on expressions of public interest, but a much greater one where expressions are targeted at specific individuals, organisations, or countries.

Conclusion

A key tenet of the book has been to highlight the tensions at the heart of the Olympics. Disputes over the legality of Rule 50 highlight a key tension between the publicly stated culture and values of the Olympic Movement and the reality of its operation against athlete activism. The legal and human rights analysis of Rule 50 demonstrates the existence of both a general tension between the Fundamental Principles of Olympism and their lack of protection by the law, and a very specific tension between the IOC's claims of political neutrality and the ways that this is enforced against athletes. This in turn highlights the precarious nature of *lex Olympica* and its vulnerability to challenge before national, international, and transnational courts, as it is now clear that the Olympic Charter is justiciable before these courts and can be declared incompatible with both domestic and international law.

If *lex sportiva* in general and *lex Olympica* in particular seek to operate as meaningful transnational legal systems, a greater respect for human rights is required. Olympic legal norms need to be developed in a legally robust way, or they will run the risk of being struck out or rewritten, as has happened with Rule 40 and could happen with Rule 50. Further, where the IOC seeks to convert *lex Olympica* into Olympic Law, these norms need to be compliant with international obligations. That is to say, the IOC needs to address a number of structural issues. First, the legal framework in which the IOC operates must be made more robust so that it is able to protect and respect athlete human rights *and* ensure that there is an adequate mechanism for providing remedies to affected athletes when an infringement is proved. Secondly, all necessary human rights frameworks must be complied with, including ensuring that the IOC is a signatory of all relevant human rights instruments such as the International Bill of Rights. If such an approach is taken by the IOC, then it will be able to demonstrate explicitly that it has moved from claiming to support human rights to actually supporting them.

This would not only ensure that *lex Olympica* protects the athletes that are fundamental to its existence, but that the Fundamental Principles of Olympism are brought to the forefront of the relationship between the IOC and the rest of the Olympic Movement. The result of these dialectics, these tensions, is that the relationship between *lex Olympica* and its application to athletes is in need of radical recalibration. This chapter and Chapter 3, with its focus on commercialisation, have provided neat illustrations of examples of the need for recalibration of the IOC-athlete relationship to be more in favour of the athletes. In the final chapter, the conclusion, we look at this recalibration not just in terms of the micro, but also the macro, and consider how this reimagining might take place in terms of the Olympic movement more generally.

Notes

1 IOC (2022) *IOC Strategic Framework on Human Rights*, available at: https://stillmed.olympics.com/media/Documents/Beyond-the-Games/Human-Rights/IOC-Strategic-Framework-on-Human-Rights.pdf (last accessed 24/02/2023).
2 Abanazir, C (2023) *Political Expression in Sport Transnational Challenges, Moral Defences* (Routledge, London).
3 See Gift, T and Miner, A (2017) 'Dropping the Ball. The Understudied Nexus of Sport and Politics' 180(1) *World Affairs* 127–161 and Barnier, A, Kelly, J and Lee J W (eds) (2017) *Routledge Handbook of Sport and Politics* (Routledge, London).

4 See generally Houlihan, B (2003) 'Politics, Power, Policy and Sport' in Houlihan, B (ed) *Sports in Society* (Sage, London) and Houlihan, B (2000) 'Politics and Sport' in Coakley, J and Dunning, E (eds) *Handbook of Sports Studies* (Sage, London), ch 13.

5 Sikes, M, Rider, C and Llewellyn, M (eds) (2022) *Sport and Apartheid South Africa: Histories of Politics, Power, and Protest* (Routledge, London). See on cricket specifically Greenfield, S and Osborn, G (1997) 'Enough Is Enough: Race, Cricket and Protest in the UK' 30(4) *Sociological Focus* 373–383.

6 White, A (2012) 'The Olympics banned list' *New Statesman*, 12 July, available at: https://www.newstatesman.com/culture/sport/2012/07/olympics-banned-list (last accessed 15/032022).

7 London Organising Committee of the Olympic Games (2012), *London 2012 terms and conditions of ticket purchase*, at 17, copy on file with authors.

8 Kim, H-J and Yamaguchi, M (2021) 'Why Japan's 'rising sun' flag is provoking anger among some at the Olympics' *LA Times*, July 23, available at: https://www.latimes.com/world-nation/story/2021-07-23/japan-rising-sun-olympic-flag-provokes-anger (last accessed 16/02/2022).

9 The Russian athletes were forced to compete under the name and flag of the Russian Olympic Committee (CAS 2020/O/6689 *World Anti-Doping Agency v. Russian Anti-Doping Agency* p 181, ruling 4(d)). This prohibition did not apply to spectators, ruling 4(d)(iii), meaning that spectators could continue to display the Russian flag, 'Russian fans can fly flag at Olympics – but no politics please' Radio Free Europe/Radio Liberty, https://www.rferl.org/a/russia-winter-olympics-flag-ioc/28998081.html (last accessed 16/022022).

10 Cha, D (2009) 'A theory of sport and politics' 26(11) *International Journal of the History of Sport* 1581–1610.

11 Malik, K (2021) 'We need to separate sport and politics. But also recognise they are inseparable' *The Guardian*, 13 June, available at: https://www.theguardian.com/commentisfree/2021/jun/13/impossible-to-keep-politics-out-of-sport-just-as-it-should-be (last accessed 24/02/2023).

12 Cottrell, M P and Nelson, T (2010) 'Not Just the Games? Power, Protest and Politics at the Olympics' 17(4) *European Journal of International Relations* 729–753, at 733.

13 Kluch, Y (2020) '"My Story Is My Activism!": (Re-)Definitions of Social Justice Activism among Collegiate Athlete Activists' 8(4–5) *Communication and Sport* 566–590, at 571, quoting Bell, L A (2016) 'Theoretical Foundations for Social Justice Education' in Adams, M, Bell, L A and Griffin, P (eds) *Teaching for Diversity and Social Justice* (Taylor & Francis, New York), 1–14.

14 Cooper, J, Macaulay, C and Rodriguez, S (2019) 'Race and Resistance: A Typology of African American Sport Activism' 54 *International Review for the Sociology of Sport* 151–181, at 172.

15 For example, in 1906 at the subsequently 'disowned' 10th Anniversary Games, Peter O'Connor replaced the Union Flag with the Irish Tricolour in protest at Irish athletes being forced to compete as part of Team GB. See further Rowbottom, M (2016) 'Čáslavská the courageous, whose Mexico Games protest took its place in a proud history' *Inside the Games*, 4 September, available at: https://www.insidethegames.biz/articles/1041218/caslavska-the-courageous-whose-mexico-games-protest-took-its-place-in-a-proud-history (last accessed 26/01/2022).

16 Nittle, N K (2021) 'Why Black American Athletes Raised Their Fists at the 1968 Olympics' *The History Channel*, 25 May, available at: https://www.history.com/news/black-athletes-raise-fists-1968-olympics (last accessed 02/02/2022).

17 Lee Evans' obituary (2021) *The Times*, 20 May, available at: https://www.thetimes.co.uk/article/lee-evans-obituary-2hbn7tt28 (last accessed 29/03/2022).

18 Hall of Fame biographies for Carlos available at: https://www.teamusa.org/Hall-of-Fame/Hall-of-Fame-Members/John-Carlos and Smith available at: https://www.teamusa.org/Hall-of-Fame/Hall-of-Fame-Members/Tommie-Smith (last accessed 02/03/2022).

19 Australian Olympic Committee (2018) 'Peter Norman's family to accept Olympic Order of Merit tonight' available at: https://www.olympics.com.au/news/peter-normans-family-to-accept-olympic-order-of-merit-tonight/ (last accessed 02/03/2022).

20 Čáslavská's Olympic biography, available at: https://www.olympedia.org/athletes/29115 (last accessed 02/03/2022).

21 Hall of Fame biography for Evans, available at: https://usopm.org/lee-evans/ (last accessed 02/03/2022).

22 Anon (2019) 'US Olympic medallist faces discipline for taking knee after winning Pan-Am gold' *The Guardian*, 11 August, available at: https://www.theguardian.com/sport/2019/aug/10/race-imboden-kneels-national-anthem-pan-am-games (last accessed 13/02/2022).

23 Bach, T (2020) *New Year's Message* 2020, available at: https://olympics.com/ioc/news/new-year-s-message-2020 (last accessed 15/02/2022).

24 IOC (2020) *Rule 50 Guidelines*, available at: https://stillmedab.olympic.org/media/Document%20Library/OlympicOrg/News/2020/01/Rule-50-Guidelines-Tokyo-2020.pdf (last accessed 15/02/2022).

25 Terraz, T (2014) '(A)Political games? Ubiquitous nationalism and the IOC's hypocrisy' available at: https://www.asser.nl/SportsLaw/Blog/post/a-political-games-ubiquitous-nationalism-and-the-ioc-s-hypocrisy (last accessed 02/03/2022).

26 IOC (1956) *Olympic Charter*, available at: https://stillmed.olympic.org/media/Document%20Library/OlympicOrg/Olympic-Studies-Centre/List-of-Resources/Official-Publications/Olympic-Charters/EN-1956-Olympic-Charter.pdf (last accessed 15/02/2022).

27 Ibid, Part VII, at 77.

28 Barker, P (2020) 'The forbidden Olympic table' *Inside the Games*, 24 January, available at: https://www.insidethegames.biz/articles/1089574/history-of-medal-tables-at-olympics (last accessed 02/03/2022).

29 Terraz, T (2014) '(A)Political games? Ubiquitous nationalism and the IOC's hypocrisy' available at: https://www.asser.nl/SportsLaw/Blog/post/a-political-games-ubiquitous-nationalism-and-the-ioc-s-hypocrisy (last accessed 02/03/2022).

30 For an examination of nationalisms in sport, see Wigham, S (ed) (2010) 'Sport and Nationalism: Theoretical Perspectives' 24(11) *Sport in Society* – special issue.

31 Terraz, T (2014) '(A)Political games? Ubiquitous nationalism and the IOC's hypocrisy' available at: https://www.asser.nl/SportsLaw/Blog/post/a-political-games-ubiquitous-nationalism-and-the-ioc-s-hypocrisy (last accessed 02/03/2022).

32 Tomizawa, R (2016) 'Vincent Matthews and Wayne Collett: A most casual protest with most striking consequences' available at: https://theolympians.co/2016/11/18/vincent-matthews-and-wayne-collett-a-most-casual-protest-with-most-striking-consequences/ (last accessed 18/02/2022)

33 Duval, A (2018) 'The Olympic Charter: A Transnational Constitution without a State?' *Journal of Law and Society* 245–269, at 253.

34 IOC (2021) *Olympic Charter*, available at: https://olympics.com/ioc/olympic-charter (last accessed 24/02/2023).

35 Little, C (2015) 'No black armbands please, but we have a rock for that' *Faster-skier*, 8 June, available at: https://fasterskier.com/2015/06/no-black-armbands-but-we-have-a-rock-for-that/ (last accessed 18/02/2022).

36 James, M and Osborn, G (2014) 'IOC rules at Sochi go too far with ban on black armbands' *The Conversation*, 21 February, available at: https://theconversation.com/ioc-rules-at-sochi-go-too-far-with-ban-on-black-armbands-23555 (last accessed 18/02/2022).

37 Smith, D (2016) 'Feyisa Lilesa: Being an athlete allowed me to be the voice of my people' *The Guardian*, 14 September, available at: https://www.theguardian.com/world/2016/sep/14/feyisa-lilesa-being-an-athlete-allowed-me-to-be-the-voice-of-my-people (last accessed 18/02/2022).

38 See https://olympics.com/athlete365/who-we-are/athletes-declaration/ (last accessed 18/02/2022).

39 Bach, T (2020) *New Year's Message 2020*, available at: https://olympics.com/ioc/news/new-year-s-message-2020 (last accessed 15/02/2022).

40 IOC, *Rule 50 Guidelines (Tokyo 2020)*, available at: https://olympics.com/athlete365?attachment_id=45550 (last accessed 02/03/2022).

41 IOC Athletes' Commission (2021) *IOC AC Athlete Expression Report*, available at: https://olympics.com/athlete365?attachment_id=35902 (last accessed 02/03/2022).

42 IOC Athletes' Commission (2021) *IOC AC Athlete Expression Report*, available at: https://olympics.com/athlete365?attachment_id=35902 (last accessed 02/03/2022), at 3.

43 Grohmann, K (2021) 'Taking a knee, raising a fist to be punished at Tokyo Games-IOC' *Reuters*, 21 April, available at: https://www.reuters.com/lifestyle/sports/taking-knee-raising-fist-be-punished-tokyo-games-ioc-2021-04-21/ (last accessed 02/03/2022).

44 FINA (2021), 'FINA confirms athlete expression opportunities for Tokyo 2020' 7 July 2021, available at: https://www.fina.org/news/2185484/fina-confirms-athlete-expression-opportunities-for-tokyo-2020/// (last accessed 02/03/2022).

45 Robinson, M (2020) 'A letter to Team USA athletes' 10 December, available at: https://www.teamusa.org/USA-Wrestling/Features/2020/December/10/Letter-to-Team-USA-athletes (last accessed 02/03/2022).

46 Anon (2021) 'Raven Saunders throws up X on podium to represent where the "oppressed meet"' *The Guardian*, 1 August, available at: https://www.theguardian.com/sport/2021/aug/01/raven-saunders-x-gesture-olympic-podium-tokyo-2020-shot-put (last accessed 18/02/2022).

47 Elliott, S (2013) 'Merchandise uses Olympics principles against Russian anti-gay laws' *New York Times*, 2 December, available at: https://www.nytimes.com/2013/12/02/business/media/merchandise-uses-olympics-principles-against-russian-anti-gay-laws.html (last accessed 11/01/2023). On the impact of the Principle 6 campaign, see Athlete Ally (2014) 'P6 campaign continues to make a difference' available at: https://www.athleteally.org/p6-campaign-continues-make-difference/ (last accessed 11/01/2023).

48 See also Anmol, J (2020) 'Political Speech in Sports: A Case for Non-Prohibition' 2(1) *Journal for Sports Law, Policy and Governance* 61–73, at 71.

49 For further details on these acts of activism, see James, M (2023), 'Restricting Athletes' Voices: The Evolution of Rule 50 and Its Application at Tokyo 2020 and Beyond' in Rook, W and Heerdt, D (eds) (2023), *Handbook on Mega-Sporting Events and Human Rights* (Routledge, London), ch 41.

50 International Judo Federation (2021) 'Fethi Nourine and Amar Benikhlef: Disciplinary Decision' available at https://www.ijf.org/news/show/fethi-nourine-and-amar-benikhlef-disciplinary-decision (last accessed 02/03/2022).

51 Anon (2021) 'Chinese champions wear Mao badges on cycling podium' *Reuters*, 2 August, available at: https://www.reuters.com/lifestyle/sports/chinese-champions-wear-mao-badges-cycling-podium-2021-08-02/ (last accessed 29/03/2022).

52 Anon (2021) 'China says no more Mao badges after IOC warning' *BBC*, 7 August, available at: https://www.bbc.co.uk/news/world-asia-china-58127804 (last accessed 29/03/2022).

53 Anon (2021) 'Raven Saunders throws up X on podium to represent where the 'oppressed meet' *The Guardian*, 1 August, available at: https://www.theguardian.com/sport/2021/aug/01/raven-saunders-x-gesture-olympic-podium-tokyo-2020-shotput (last accessed 18/02/2022).

54 Scully, R (2021) 'US Olympic fencers wear pink masks to protest against teammate accused of sexual assault' *The Hill*, 30 July, available at: https://thehill.com/policy/international/565734-us-olympic-fencers-wear-pink-masks-to-protest-teammate-accused-of-sexual (last accessed 02/03/2022).

55 Die Welt (2021) '"The only right thing:" Hockey's Nike Lorenz allowed to wear rainbow band' 22 July, available at: https://www.dw.com/en/the-only-right-thing-hockeys-nike-lorenz-allowed-to-wear-rainbow-band/a-58610913 (last accessed 02/03/2022).

56 Kyodo News (2021) 'Britain, Chile women's Olympic soccer teams take knee before games opener' 21 July, available at: https://english.kyodonews.net/news/2021/07/d2ac575d4ad7-britain-chile-womens-olympic-soccer-teams-take-knee-before-games-opener.html (last accessed 02/03/2022).

57 Grell, T (2018) 'The International Olympic Committee and Human Rights Reforms: Game Changer or Mere Window Dressing?' 17(3–4) *International Sports Law Journal* 160–169.

58 IAAF (2019), 'IAAF publishes briefing notes and Q&A on female eligibility regulations' 7 May, available at: https://www.iaaf.org/news/press-release/questions-answers-iaaf-female-eligibility-reg (last accessed 02/03/2022).

59 Di Marco, A (2021) 'Athletes' Freedom of Expression: The Relative Political Neutrality of Sport' 21 *Human Rights Law Review* 620–640, and James, M and Osborn, G (2023, forthcoming) 'Athlete Activism at the Olympics: Challenging the Legality of Rule 50 as a Restriction on Freedom of Expression' in Boillet, V, Weerts S and Zeigler, A (eds), *Human Rights in Sport* (Springer Nature).

60 Ingle, S (2021) 'Algerian judoka sent home from Olympics after refusing to face Israeli' *The Guardian*, 24 July, available at: https://www.theguardian.com/sport/2021/jul/24/algerian-judoka-sent-home-from-olympics-after-refusing-to-compete-against-israeli (last accessed 18/02/2022).

61 Shahlaei, F (2017) 'When Sports Stand against Human Rights: Regulating Restrictions on Athlete Speech in the Global Sports Arena' 38(1) Loyola of Los Angeles Entertainment Law Review 99–120.

62 *Mutu and Pechstein v. Switzerland*, applications nos. 40575/10 and 67474/10, available at: https://hudoc.echr.coe.int/eng#{%22fulltext%22:(%22pechstein%22),%22itemid%22:(%22001-186828%22)} (last accessed 24/02/2023) and Goertz, D (2020) 'Recap of the Pechstein saga: A hot potato in the hands of the sports arbitration community' available at: http://arbitrationblog.kluwerarbitration.com/2020/02/01/recap-of-the-pechstein-saga-a-hot-potato-in-the-hands-of-the-sports-arbitration-community/ (last accessed 24/02/2023).

63 As CAS has its seat in Switzerland, all CAS arbitrations are governed by Swiss arbitration law, specifically Chapter 12 of the Swiss Private International Law Act.

64 James, M (2017), *Sports Law* (Palgrave Macmillan), 63–64.

65 Duval, A (2022) 'Lost in Translation? The European Convention on Human Rights at the Court of Arbitration for Sport' 22 *International Sports Law Journal* 132–151.

66 *Fenerbahce SK v. UEFA* (CAS 2013/A/3139) par. 88–89, 5 December 2013.

67 *Dink v. Turkey*, application nos. 2668/07, 6102/08, 30079/08, 7072/09 and 7124/09, par. 106 et seq.

68 Everington, K (2021) 'Taiwan's national flag anthem played in front of Chinese athletes for 1st time' *Taiwan News*, 2 August, available at: https://www.taiwannews.com.tw/en/news/4262639 (last accessed 16/03/2022).

69 Di Marco, A (2021) 'Athletes' Freedom of Expression: The Relative Political Neutrality of Sport' 21 *Human Rights Law Review* 620–640.
70 Summarised in *Stoll v. Switzerland*, application no. 69698/01, para. 101, and restated in <u>Morice</u> *v. France* application no. 29369/10 at para. 124.
71 *Palomo Sanchex and others v. Spain* (applications nos. 28955/06, 28957/06, 28959/06 and 28964/06).
72 Application no. 20373/17, *Josip Šimunić v. Croatia*, available at: https://hudoc.echr.coe.int/fre#{%22itemid%22:(%22001-189769%22)} (last accessed 15/03/2022).

5 Recalibrating the Olympics: Misplaced Leverage and a Relational Turn?

Introduction

In the previous four chapters, we have analysed the impact of the tensions that strain the relationships between the International Olympic Committee (IOC) and key stakeholders in the Olympic Movement, in particular the athletes. The focus of our analyses has been through a legal lens that identifies when these tensions reach a breaking point such that they can only be resolved by legal action. This has already happened in respect of the commercial restrictions imposed on athletes by Rule 40(3) of the Olympic Charter (Rule 40), though its partial resolution will likely lead to further tensions in the medium term, and is on the cusp of happening in respect of the restrictions placed on athlete activism by Rule 50 of the Olympic Charter (Rule 50). To avoid further examination of the legality of *lex Olympica*, the root cause of these tensions needs to be negotiated differently. Whilst the law may have some impact in ameliorating the problems caused by the tensions that we've identified, legal action should be considered to be a last resort. In this final chapter, it is argued that further recalibration of the IOC's relationships is needed, and we propose a potential framework within which these negotiations could take place. To orientate the reader, this chapter begins with a brief review of our approach so far in order to contextualise the conclusions ultimately reached.

Our point of departure was to identify a series of tensions, including those in the IOC's key relationships, in particular, with the athletes. We illustrated throughout that there is too great a focus on protecting the commercial rights and income streams of the IOC and the local organising committee of each edition of the Olympic Games, and not enough respect for the values embedded in the Fundamental Principles of Olympism. We then demonstrated how this tension is magnified by the *lex Olympica* that has been created to define and protect those commercial rights being prioritised through the process of forced transplantation into national law as Olympic law. In contrast, the promotion of Olympism as the underpinning culture of the Olympic Movement remains governed more informally by *lex Olympica* and the empty threat of invoking Rule 33 of the Olympic Charter (Rule 33) for any breaches of

DOI: 10.4324/9780429323355-5

the legal covenant provided by the host government in its Candidate City File. These concepts were introduced in Chapters 1 and 2, which laid the groundwork for a more detailed analysis of two specific areas of contestation in Chapters 3 and 4, and the law's impact on the evolution of these Olympic relationships. First, the tension between the prioritisation of the commercial rights of the IOC and the local organising committee over the right of the athletes to maximise their earnings potential from playing sport was considered. This analysis demonstrated how a successful legal challenge to the restrictions imposed on athletes by Rule 40 of the Olympic Charter (Rule 40) resulted in the rewriting of Rule 40 and the accompanying guidance issued by the IOC and the National Olmypic Committees (NOCs). In other words, the operation of national law and EU law in Germany created change in the *lex Olympica* in a way that reduced the tension and promoted a more respectful relationship between the two sides. Secondly, we examined the tension between the IOC's public statements on respecting and protecting human rights with the restrictions that it imposes on the freedom of expression of athletes competing at the Games under Rule 50 of the Olympic Charter (Rule 50). The analysis demonstrated that, once again, the law could be utilised to challenge the legality of *lex Olympica* before national and transnational courts and force the IOC to go beyond its claim that it respects and protects human rights, by ensuring that it must comply with international human rights instruments and provide remedies for situations where it has breached its obligations.

This final chapter draws together these analyses and provides an explanation of how reframing key parts of the Olympic legal framework can form the basis of a recalibration of the IOC's key relationships to create a better balance between the culture of Olympism and the commercial imperatives associated with hosting the Games. The theoretical justification for this proposition is that by adopting a more contextual approach to the contracts governing the IOC's relationships with its key stakeholders, as envisaged by relational contract theory, more equal and less asymmetrical relationships will evolve that are underpinned by Olympism instead of profit maximisation for the IOC and local organising committee. A more pragmatic justification can also be offered: a failure to recalibrate these inherent tensions, to reassert the role of Olympism, and to provide an effective means of promoting, respecting, and remedying breaches of internationally recognised human rights will result in these changes being forced on the IOC. Successful legal challenges will either require the IOC to recalibrate its rules, or it will need to relocate to a more pliant jurisdiction, with the loss of credibility that will entail.

Without these recalibrations, it can no longer be taken as read, if it ever could, that the Olympic Games is a force for good. Indeed, there is a growing movement pushing for its abolition, as can be seen through the work of the NOlympics movement and others with an anti-Olympic ethos.[1] In 2012, Lenskyj, a well-known Olympic critic, reviewed the issues that the IOC and Olympic officials had tried to address, including leadership, transparency, accountability, social responsibility, and sporting mythology. She found that the IOC had largely failed in its attempts to implement change, which represents a significant lost opportunity to regain credibility.[2] When considering various anti-Olympic campaigns, including those against the candidatures of Tokyo, Chicago, and Athens, Zervas wrote despairingly of the seeming inability of the IOC to change, arguing:

> The only viable solution would be an Olympic *revolution*, either internal or external. The internal revolution would be a complete reform of the IOC and of the Olympic Games towards a less commercialised, less wealth-centred structure.[3]

The previous chapters have examined this issue of the over-commercialisation of the Olympics and the tensions that this has created, particularly between the culture of Olympism and the commercial imperatives of hosting. These chapters have argued that the IOC's approach needs rethinking, or as Zervas would argue, revolutionising. Currently, the IOC's commercial interests are overly provided for, with only lip service paid to its own underpinning philosophy of Olympism. If support for the IOC and the Olympic Games is not going to diminish further than it has already as a result of it requiring special dispensation for its members in normal times, insisting that the Games go ahead during a global pandemic, and acting hypocritically over athlete activism, then it needs to pay more attention to promoting its values, both in respect of its relationship with the athletes and with host cities and nations. To do this, as Zervas hints, the IOC will need to reassess very carefully its values, and in particular, what it means to be an Olympic host. *This will require serious and sustained change.*

On a very basic level, the extreme options are to abolish the Olympic Games completely, or to do nothing at all. What we are proposing here is a pragmatic middle ground more akin to Zervas' internal revolution. Working on the basis that three major economies will be hosting the next three editions of the Summer Games in Paris 2024, Los Angeles 2028, and Brisbane 2032, it is extremely likely that they will go ahead in some form. Therefore, a recalibration of the key relationships affected by the Games is needed as a matter of urgency. In Chapters 3 and 4, the focus was on the athlete, but similar arguments can be put forward for the need to reform and refocus the relationships with the Host Cities, and wider communities within the host nation, in particular. There have been many calls for recalibration:

> What's needed is a root-and-branch rethinking that begins with reality rather than fantasy. Starry-eyed talk about how the Olympics promote peace, foster a spirit of global friendship, and combat discrimination should be set aside in favor of an evidence-based calculation of the social, environmental, and financial costs of staging the events and the ways athletes are treated, from early training grounds to the victory podium.[4]

A crucial part of this rethinking is examining how the tension between culture and commerce can be recalibrated, and how the Olympics can become more inclusive. The modern Olympics was founded on exclusivity at various levels, but in the 21st century the lack of multiculturalism within the Olympic ethos is striking. Parry argues that Olympic practices should be decentralised and makes suggestions including radically rethinking the programme of events.[5] Some of these themes are echoed in the IOC's own Agenda 2020 reforms and are often couched in terms of positive legacies; however, the positive benefits of hosting the Games have been subject to fierce criticisms.[6]

What we propose here is a means of undertaking this recalibration by using two distinct theoretical tools that enable us to consider different approaches going forward. First, we examine how the IOC has misused the leverage that it has over other stakeholders by focusing exclusively on the need to protect its own revenue streams. The issue of leverage by the dominant contracting party, and the asymmetry that this creates, concludes that the IOC needs to use this leverage differently, or must create new leverage by actually walking, and not just talking, the Fundamental Principles of Olympism and a commitment to human rights protections. It can then be seen as a facilitator of change, instead of acting in an overtly and commercially protectionist and self-serving manner.

Secondly, we explore how the concept of relational contract theory might be used as a framework for developing a different approach to easing the tension between what the IOC is supposed to stand for and what, in reality, it appears to be standing for.[7] As the basis of *lex Olympica* and the source of the key Olympic legal norms is a framework of interlocking contracts, including in particular the Olympic Charter and the Olympic Host Contract, the use of relational contract theory as an analytical tool to redefine those norms is appropriate. We conclude this chapter, and indeed the book, by considering what this recalibration might look like, and what relationships it might affect, particularly those between the athlete and the IOC and the host nation and the IOC. First, though, we consider how the IOC has used its leverage, and its historically strong bargaining position, and argue that a different approach here could alleviate the tensions we have discussed and foster a more cooperative approach going forward that might be to the IOC's advantage.

The IOC – misplaced leverage?

Despite the inclusion of some surprising terms, and inevitable friction between parties to such a major agreement, the terms of the contract have never been arbitrated or litigated. Some argue that the Host City Contract is unenforceable, but the more important and pressing question is *what, if any, is the purpose of this multi-billion dollar contract?*[8]

Table 5.1 Olympic Host and Bidders: 1996–2020[10]

Year	Host	Other Shortlisted Bids	Total Bids
1996	Atlanta	Athens, Belgrade, Manchester, Melbourne, Toronto	6
2000	Sydney	Beijing, Berlin, Istanbul, Manchester	5
2004	Athens	Buenos Aires, Cape Town, Rome, Stockholm	5
2008	Beijing	Istanbul, Osaka, Paris, Toronto	5
2012	London	Madrid, Moscow, New York City, Paris	5
2016	Rio	Chicago, Madrid, Tokyo	4
2020	Tokyo	Istanbul, Madrid	3

One of the key causes of the current asymmetry in the IOC's relationships is its misuse of the leverage that it has over other contracting parties through its focus on self-serving commercial protectionism. The ability of the IOC to dictate its legislative needs is only possible when it is in a powerful enough position to be able to exert the necessary leverage over potential hosts. This is magnified when states are attracted to host such events because of perceived soft power benefits.[9] Since 1984, when only Los Angeles was prepared to ac-commodate the Games, there have been multiple candidate cities willing to bid for the right to host the summer edition of the Olympics (Table 5.1). In situations such as this, the IOC's demands can become extensive and will in general be met by prospective hosts with little question, opposition, or debate. Where conditions are such that there is a more limited field of candidates, or where bidding cities are seen as being inappropriate in some way, then it is more difficult for the IOC to insist on its conditions being met.

As can be seen, over this period the IOC was in a position of strength. For each edition of the Games, there were several viable potential hosts and, theo-retically at least, this should work in the IOC's favour in terms of being able to exact the contractual terms that it wants from the eventual winner. An anal-ogy can be drawn with other legal relationships where there is an imbalance or asymmetry in bargaining power. In the music industry, for example, there are generally more artists wanting recording contracts than record companies can afford to, or would wish to, contract with. As Greenfield and Osborn have argued:

> This operational model, demanding a constant supply of artists, places record companies in a superior bargaining position with respect to the artists, conferring upon them much greater leverage. Contracts thus tend to be asymmetrical in that they tend to reflect the needs of the record company first and foremost.[11]

Any asymmetry leads to the potential for the party with the stronger bargaining power to use their leverage in a self-regarding way, something memorably explained by Lord Diplock as a 'take it or leave it' approach, where there is scant opportunity for negotiating contentious or problematic terms.[12] The requirement that Olympic athletes submit to the exclusive jurisdiction of the Court of Arbitration for Sport (CAS) has been similarly labelled, with the forced arbitration clauses contained in athlete participation agreements being held to be non-consensual, resulting in additional procedural safeguards being required at CAS hearings.[13]

Within the context of Olympic bids, such an imbalance can also be seen where there are multiple viable candidate cities all striving for the same prize – the hosting of the Games. When this occurs, the IOC can leverage its strengthened bargaining position to exact the extensive terms and conditions that it wants. Where the relationship becomes more symmetrical, however, notions of leverage become much less important. The fewer the bidders, or the less financially, socially, and/or politically attractive the prize is perceived as being, the less leverage the IOC is able to exert. Much like the situation a record company may find itself in when there are no other players in the field and a number of artists are keen to be signed by the company, the IOC can utilise this asymmetrical relationship to exact the promises and terms it desires safe in the knowledge that the putative host cities will do whatever is necessary to accommodate them.

July 2015 brought into focus the declining leverage that the IOC can exert on prospective hosts. Following the need to reopen the competition for the design of the logo for the Tokyo 2020 Games on the grounds that the original winner had been accused of plagiarism,[14] the much more significant blow to the IOC's leverage was when Boston withdrew its candidacy to host the 2024 Games.[15] Boston's refusal to underwrite the financial commitment to host the Games came after the high-profile withdrawals from the race to host the 2022 Winter Olympics. With the subsequent withdrawals of Hamburg, Rome, and Budapest, the underlying concern for the IOC was that it was losing leverage by being unable to assemble the usual field of four to six candidates to provide a genuine choice for the final vote, a position epitomised when having to choose Beijing over Almaty for the 2022 Winter Games. An examination of the bidding context demonstrates a marked shift over the next three editions of the Games. In particular, the 2024 process was a watershed. When three of the candidate cities withdrew, an extraordinary IOC Session in July 2017 resulted in the decision to allow the two remaining bidders for the 2024 Games to be invited to host in 2024 (Paris) and 2028 (Los Angeles). Previously, the most extreme example of the IOC's lack of leverage occurred during the bidding for the 1984 Summer Games. As the sole bidder, the Los Angeles organising committee was able to refuse one of the IOC's fundamental obligations for hosting the Olympics – that the host city municipality financially underwrite the cost of organising the Games. More recently, the competition to host the 2022 Winter Games saw all of the IOC's preferred bidders withdraw, most of them in reaction to a combination of escalating costs and the peripheral demands being made of them.[16] This left a depleted field of two: Beijing (the ultimate choice) and Almaty, both of which have dubious human rights records.

The 2022 process was described by Gauthier as nothing short of disastrous.[17] Where the field is limited in this way, the IOC is unable to exert its usual levels of leverage. In response to this potential loss of power, the IOC adopted the Agenda 2020 reforms.[18] Nevertheless, similar problems arose with the 2024 bidding process, resulting in a reconsideration of the way that candidate cities bid to host the Games, and a new process was approved at the IOC Session in Lausanne on 24 June 2019. These proposals included establishing an ongoing dialogue to explore interest in hosting the Games and to create 'Future Host Commissions' to oversee this process. To enable these new Commissions to function effectively, bye-law 2 was added to Rule 33 of the Olympic Charter to allow the IOC a greater flexibility of approach to the process of appointing a host city.[19] This was largely the result of an increasing reticence to host the Games on the IOC's terms. The 2024 bidding process began with Paris, Hamburg, Budapest, Rome, and Los Angeles all becoming candidate cities, but was beset with withdrawals, uncertainty, and the threat of unfavourable, or actually unfavourable, outcomes of referenda on whether to host the Games.[20]

Agenda 2020 can be seen as the start of the IOC attempting to regain its position of strength by reinforcing the positive aspects of the Olympic project. The IOC sees it as a strategic roadmap for the Olympic Movement and that '[t]he 40 recommendations are like pieces of a jigsaw puzzle that, when put together, form a picture of the IOC safeguarding the uniqueness of the Olympic Games and strengthening sport in society.'[21] In particular, it now requires that legacy issues are embedded explicitly into the bid documentation from the outset as this '... has been recognised by the IOC as a persuasive notion for gaining public support for and demonstrating public benefit from staging the Games.'[22] That these issues had become central was demonstrated by the fact that the first two Agenda 2020 working groups were those investigating the 'Bidding Procedure' and 'Sustainability and Legacy.'[23] This ensured that the IOC was '[leaving] no doubt as to the sources of immediate concern, so too each successive defection from the contest for the 2022 Winter Games increased pressure on IOC members to respect the Agenda 2020 process and to anticipate real change.'[24]

Notwithstanding the implementation of Agenda 2020, the result of the IOC's misuse of its leverage, by focusing on commerce instead of culture, and its inability to exert its leverage effectively where there is a lack of viable options to host the Olympics has brought us to a place where the key Olympic relationships need recalibrating. This will ensure that the imbalance between the IOC's commercial demands does not undermine the ability of athletes to earn a living from sport, that Olympism and human rights are promoted alongside commercial rights, and that there is an increased cooperation between the

IOC and the host. To achieve this recalibration, a new approach to governing the IOC's relationships can be found, using relational contract theory as a starting point to frame a new approach.

Relationality and recalibration

To ensure that the relationship between the IOC and the athletes can be rebalanced effectively and appropriately, it is essential to alleviate the tensions between the IOC and the host. A further justification for the need to recalibrate the IOC's relationship with the athletes is found in the behaviour of 'pliant states' that have in place a hosting strategy for mega and major sporting events.[25] This group includes not only the confirmed future hosts that have promised to implement new Olympic laws that protect event organisers' commercial rights, but also potential candidate cities and host countries that offer these protections pre-emptively through generic, as opposed to event-specific, legislation. This latter group is additionally problematic in that these generic laws have the potential to subvert full parliamentary scrutiny, as the laws have been implemented already, making them particularly attractive to mega sports events rights holders. This problem is exacerbated by an imbalance, or asymmetry, existing between the two contracting parties. The problem reflects the dialectics we refer to in Chapter 1, and the tension between the IOC's requirements and the impact that they have on the host nation is palpable. As Louw puts it:

> When we place the various elements of the *sui generis* commercial protection of events in the proverbial scales of justice, there appears to be a significant imbalance. On the one side we find draconian prohibitions and substantial civil and criminal penalties for insufficiently blameworthy conduct and a lack of requirement of actual harm for those in whose interest such legislation is enacted and enforced. On the other side we find often severe curtailment of civil liberties. How can this *status quo* be in the public interest?[26]

What is clear is that event laws are contentious enough when implemented to protect specific events with bespoke legislation, but even more problematic when of generic application to any event considered to be worthy of protection by a pliant government. We previously outlined a series of critiques of generic legislation, including the fact that it often creates more difficulties than it solves.[27] More worryingly, there is a danger that governments become subservient to the commercial whims of sponsors and provide the conditions of a 'pliant state.' In addition, without individual scrutiny and accountability and devoid of any ongoing parliamentary oversight, the particularities of each specific event are occluded. Further evidence of the normalisation of these protections is their application beyond the Olympic Games to events including the FIFA World Cup and the Commonwealth Games, thereby fundamentally extending the potential scope of *lex Olympica* and fuelling the normalisation process through the socialisation of the transplanted laws. In a broader sense, this normalisation of the exceptional exacerbates the problems caused by *lex Olympica* with a generalised application of major event law.

A strong argument can be maintained that a more cooperative model, taking into account the needs of both parties and predicated on a more collaborative approach, would be preferable and perhaps ameliorate some of the tensions that we have outlined. To illustrate this, we use relational contract theory as a lens to provide a novel approach to recalibrating the relationship between the IOC and the athletes. Relational contract theory is a response to the problems of classical contract theory and specifically an attack on a view of contract law that does not consider broader contextual factors: '[the] more classical contract law was placed in context, the less sense it made.'[28] Recent years have seen the approach move from the theoretical to the practical with the theory being utilised by the courts increasing its visibility.[29] Arguably a more relational approach, particularly in the sense of its privileging of issues of reciprocity and cooperation, might be the answer to some of the problems associated with bidding for and hosting major events.

At present, the relationship between the IOC and the athletes and the IOC and the hosts is imbalanced and asymmetrical. The IOC can impose its will on other contracting parties, in a 'take it or leave it' approach, because of the desire, or desperation, of the hosts to host the Olympics and the athletes to perform at the Games. Morin and Gold argue that legal transplants are particularly problematic in situations that involve such asymmetry.[30] Asymmetry has been examined previously in respect of the application of relational contract theory[31] and is equally applicable to the relationships between the IOC and its key stakeholders. A specific example of this asymmetry being operationalised was when the IOC refused a second postponement of Tokyo 2020, relying on the terms of the HCC to override the wishes of the Japanese government and its people.

Whilst relational contract theory is of course essentially contractual in focus, for Feinman, '[exchange], in turn, is not limited to defined monetizable exchange, but also includes other interactions in which reciprocity is a dominant element.' Using Feinman's radical rereading of relationality, it is arguable that 'an astonishingly wide range of transactions are subject to the same body of theory.'[32] For our purposes, this reciprocity is important in terms of a rebalancing of requirements and effecting change in rights holders towards a more cooperative approach. It is clear that relational contract theory can apply in a number of situations, including where the relationship between the parties is governed by the Olympic Charter, the athlete participation agreement and declaration, and the HCC. Examining the HCC through a relational lens has already been attempted by Borowick who illustrated how transactional efficiencies can be achieved through relational (and referential) mechanisms.[33] It is also clear that using some of the central tenets of relationality may allow a more cooperative and collaborative approach and provide a means for recalibrating the terms of the IOC's relationship with the athletes.

Social context is at the heart of relational contract theory, and this approach, developed from the work of Ian Macneil, has become increasingly significant.[34] Whilst Macneil may be seen as the godfather of relational theory, the work of Stewart Macaulay has been extremely significant in its evolution.[35] A key issue is the original purpose of the relationship:

> In the relational view of Macaulay and Macneil, parties treat their contracts more like marriages than like one night stands. Obligations grow out of the commitment that they have made to one another, and the conventions that the trading community establishes for such commitments; they are not frozen at the initial moment of commitment, but change as circumstances change; the object of contracting is not primarily to allocate risks, but to signify a commitment to cooperate.[36]

Macaulay argues that relational agreements require not so much a meeting of minds over specific details, but over a broader commitment:

> Relational contracts, typically, are not specific and precise allocations of risk. They involve complex transactions, and often it is hard to determine when they begin and are to end. *They are agreements to cooperate to achieve mutually desired goals* [our emphasis].[37]

This idea of mutually desired goals is an interesting one. It can be argued that rather than privileging commercial protections for the sponsors, public investment in the event needs to be acknowledged and protected equally. This can be framed as giving something back, or in contractual terms, ensuring reciprocity, or symmetrical responsibilities. Thus, in relational terms, sports mega events not only have the potential to effect positive change in the host, but can facilitate a reciprocal or symbiotic change *in the rights holder too*. It is not, therefore, just change on the part of the potential host that can be effected, but also change in the body that traditionally insists on these legal requirements being implemented for its own benefit – the IOC.

Frydlinger et al. make the point that traditional contracts often fail. Having provided various examples of dysfunctional or unsatisfactory contractual practice, they provide a framework for increasing the relationality of a contract. First, take time to lay the foundations so that both parties make a conscious attempt to create an environment of trust. Secondly, co-create a shared vision and objectives to keep expectations aligned in a changing environment. Thirdly, adopt guiding principles that provide a methodology of reciprocity, autonomy, honesty, loyalty, equity, and integrity. Fourthly, align expectations and interests. Finally, stay aligned.[38] Although it could be argued that Agenda 2020 has incorporated the first two of these into the bidding process, in general these key elements of operationalising relational contract theory in the IOC's relationships have been ignored. A more relational approach could include, for example, new ways of addressing human rights challenges by focussing on greater collective action.[39] Further, it could mean facilitating more responsible business practices by the rights holders by requiring adherence to the United Nations Guiding Principles on Human Rights in Business (UNGPs)[40] and sharing good practice not only with future organisers of the Olympic Games, but with the wider Olympic Movement as a whole.[41] The underlying principles of relational theory fit well here, privileging cooperation at the expense of competition and trying to reach a mutually beneficial position that focuses on preserving ongoing relationships in their wider contexts. Thus, relational contract theory could be used to justify a recalibration of the IOC's key relationships. This in turn could reduce the tensions identified and initiate a movement towards increased symmetry in the allocation of power. It is this that we will be using to justify our conclusions on ways forward.

We have used the lens of relational contract theory to suggest that a different approach to hosting events, to contractual practice and 'bargaining' for such events, may provide a necessary counterbalance that can tackle the asymmetry and leverage issues we have identified above. In this way, relationality can be used to inform a recalibration of the relationship between the parties by taking into account the *context of the event* and the wishes and needs of *all* parties through a process that promotes mutuality of interests. The Arup *Cities Alive* report[42] noted that reinvention of the concept of legacy was potentially important and could impact upon the expectations and requirements of both the host and the IOC.[43] Schnitzer and Haizinger[44] analyse the likely impact of Agenda 2020 on future Games and its potential benefits (for example, increased cost-effectiveness, reduced operational requirements, selection of venues made more flexible, and the legacy secured during the life cycle of the event) stressing that sustainability is key. Their analysis provides a useful roadmap of what a relational recalibration might look like and notes that Agenda 2020 is partly the catalyst for this.

One of the key issues that emerges from our analysis above is that the historic imbalance of bargaining power, of asymmetry in the relationships, has led to onerous conditions being required of athletes and hosts; a more relational approach will help recalibrate these asymmetries into relationships grounded in mutuality. Our proposal is that there needs to be a rebalancing of the relationships that exist. There is already some useful good practice in evidence, such as increased acknowledgment of human rights commitments, but relational contract theory could enable *lex Olympica* to become a tool to drive a meaningful change.

Ultimately, any recalibration can be undertaken in many ways, but the essence would be that it forms part of a reciprocal relationship. In relation to the hosts, this could include the event organisers being required to justify the need for the protective laws, rather than simply claiming that they are necessary, requiring a profit-sharing scheme between the state and organisers, accepting that there is a symbiotic relationship between the host and the event, and ensuring that Olympism is utilised as a guiding framework. In relation to the athletes, it should include a greater role for genuinely independent representative bodies of athletes, whether in the form of unions or commissions, collective bargaining agreements covering marketing and income redistribution, and the effective implementation of the 'protect, respect and remedy' framework for human rights protection founded in the UNGPs.

Embedding relationality in the IOC's relationships

This book began with the premise that the Olympics divides and that there is a series of tensions at the heart of the Olympic Movement. In particular, we argued that there is a fundamental tension between the commercial imperatives of hosting the Olympic Games and the cultural underpinning and philosophy of Olympism and that the balance between these opposing forces is in need of re-evaluation and recalibration. We have demonstrated that traditional asymmetries in its key strategic relationships with the athletes and the hosts have resulted in the IOC abusing its leverage in a number of ways. Instead of maintaining the status quo, which is likely to result in further legal defeats, the IOC must undertake a complete recalibration of its relationships with its key stakeholders. This needs to take place across all IOC activities and be embedded in the way that the Games are organised and are perceived to be organised.

Any recalibration must take into account not only that sports mega events have the potential to effect positive changes on the athletes and in the host, but can and should facilitate a reciprocal or symbiotic change *in the rights holder* too. Building on the analyses undertaken throughout this book, changes at the micro or individual level that improve athletes' rights should have the reciprocal impact of ensuring that the IOC is compliant with its inter- and transnational obligations, such as the UNGPs. Further, changes to the HCC can ensure that Olympism is operationalised in a way that reinforces the positive reasons for hosting the Games in host nations that are compliant with the underlying philosophy of the Olympic Charter.

Recalibrating the IOC's relationship with athletes

Our point of departure here is that the IOC needs to recalibrate its relationship with the athletes and to act more collaboratively with and relationally towards them. There are a number of potential benefits to this, but in particular it would be a strategic and tactical step to help ensure that athletes, who are increasingly commercially, politically, and legally aware, do not bring further challenges to the application of *lex Olympica* and Olympic law, which have the potential to damage and further erode the IOC's entrenched position. There is of course a public relations angle that the IOC could also exploit to show that it is reacting and responding to contemporary issues and a changing political and sporting landscape that it has failed to grasp fully to date. It has the added benefit that it brings the fundamental Principles of Olympism to the fore and shows that the IOC is willing to walk the talk of Agenda 2020. This could be implemented fairly easily, by embedding the protection of athletes' rights in the Olympic legal framework and ensuring that the Games are run for the athletes in consultation with the athletes.

An effective starting point would be to embed two key documents created by the World Players' Association into the *lex Olympica*. The Universal Declaration of Players' Rights is the first comprehensive articulation of athletes' rights and sets the benchmark for international sporting organisations to meet their obligations to guarantee the fundamental rights of players.[45] Drawing on a range of key international instruments, the Declaration includes specific rights that every athlete should have respected and protected: that every player has the right to work, to collectively bargain, to unionise, to share fairly in the economic activity and wealth of the sport that they have helped generate, to have their name, image, and performance protected, and that they have the right to freedom of opinion and expression. Alongside of this, the World Player Rights Policy details what sports bodies need to do to embed and embrace their responsibility towards players and ensure compliance with the UNGPs.[46] This includes commitments to act in accordance with the International Bill of Rights and without discrimination, and includes specific obligations to operationalise a binding and effective player rights policy, undertake player rights due diligence, and provide access to effective remedies.

By incorporating the Universal Declaration of Players' Rights and the World Player Rights Policy into the *lex Olympica*, the IOC would ensure that a benchmark for protecting and respecting athletes' rights with effective remedies for their infringement was established. The World Player Rights Policy could be a requirement for all International Sports Federations and National Olympic Committees, ensuring that a standard approach across sport was implemented. This would ensure that athletes' rights were taken seriously and that they had the right to unionise and to be consulted. The tension between the need for the IOC to protect its revenue streams and the athletes to earn a living would be reduced as athletes could collectively bargain to ensure an equitable distribution of the income generated by the Olympic Games. Rules 40 and 50 of the Olympic Charter, the athlete participation agreements, and the athlete declaration could all be redrafted to ensure their compliance with the Universal Declaration of Players' Rights and the World Player Rights Policy, ensuring a coherent and consistent approach to athletes' rights for the first time.

By engaging in a relational recalibration of its relationship with the athletes, the IOC is likely to secure the long-term future of the Olympic Games by ensuring that the athletes continue to want to engage with it as an event. Having examined one example of this recalibration process from the athletes' perspective, we now illustrate how this might be actualised by examining how the HCC can be relationalised, and the need to recalibrate the impact of the IOC's law-making capacity.

Recalibrating the Host City Contract

The Host City Contract is a fundamental element of the *lex Olympica*. It provides the legal framework within which the Olympics must be celebrated and includes within it the various legal requirements and guarantees that a successful candidate must implement if it is to be invited to host an edition of the Games. As a key vehicle for delivering the Games, and an exemplar of the IOC's misused leverage, it provides myriad examples of the tensions that were outlined in Chapter 1 and are, therefore, in need of recalibration. A successful, relational rewriting of the HCC will ensure not only that there is a more symmetrical relationship between the IOC and its hosts, but also that the IOC can ensure that athletes' rights are guaranteed specifically as a condition of hosting the Games.

Recent years have seen increasing dissatisfaction with many elements of the bidding and hosting process for the Olympic Games. These have centred in particular on the spiralling costs of hosting the Games in three specific areas. First, the economic costs are increasingly difficult to justify in the absence of proof of a relevant and lasting legacy, particularly in times of ongoing austerity and when cost overruns are almost inevitable.[47] Secondly, the environmental impact of the Games is being increasingly questioned; at Sochi 2014, Rio 2016, and PyeongChang 2018, Olympic venues were built on a variety of protected environments for events that held little interest for the domestic market.[48] Thirdly, the social cost of hosting the Games is being increasingly catalogued. The forced relocation of businesses in London and mass clearances of favelas in Rio are brought to the attention of the watching and increasingly critical world.[49] The combination of these factors has led to fewer bidders and a consequent loss of leverage for the IOC.

The relationship between host cities and the IOC is at the heart of the Olympic project, but this relationship is currently in a state of flux. As Gold and Gold note, for early editions of the Games IOC members tended to nominate cities in their home countries, something that appeared to work well when the burden was small and events often took place in existing, if adapted, stadia. However, as the Games evolved, this became more problematic and increasingly '...host cities were expected to act as risk-takers' on behalf of the IOC.[50] Whilst there were sufficient competing candidates willing to act as risk-takers, the IOC was able to exploit its leverage and be demanding; however, it is more difficult for the IOC to be quite so demanding when there are no viable alternative hosts. This has particularly been the case with the Winter Games, where the withdrawal of Oslo led to a damning headline in *The Independent*: 'Will Norway's refusal to meet the eye-watering demands of the IOC be the moment the world realizes only dictators can host the Olympics?'[51]

Even if this was perhaps too melodramatic, it is increasingly clear that the IOC can no longer be as demanding as it has been previously. It is not just attracting hosts for the Winter Games that is proving problematic; the field for the 2024 edition narrowed as anti-Games protests became more organised and vociferous, and the benefits of hosting were publicly contested. As noted above, Agenda 2020 was ostensibly the start of a recalibration process that would make the bidding and staging of the Games a more open and transparent process. This includes an 'invitation phase' where potential cities can enter into a dialogue with the IOC, and the bidding phase being divided into three stages that comprise the full bid. The new procedure aims at being '... supportive of potential host cities, more sensitive to their needs, reduce the cost of preparing for and staging the Games, and [encouraging] a wider variety of cities to consider applying to stage the Games.'[52] It is too early to say whether this will be successful, though it is clear that a reconsideration of Olympism, and the recalibration of the expected legal and social requirements, has not yet been adequately addressed. A relational reworking of the HCC has become essential.

The actualisation of a relational approach will be central to the future relationship between the IOC and the host. Gauthier argues that a 'progressive bidder' might be able to put into place practices that protect labour and environmental rights, for example.[53] On the other hand, the IOC may seek to question more directly the state of a prospective host's human rights and workers' rights protections and require specific guarantees that international standards are adhered to as part of future bid requirements. Conversely, sole bidders may be able to reject outright the IOC's demands when negotiating leverage is rebalanced.

A pertinent example of how a more relational approach might work was seen at the Glasgow 2014 Commonwealth Games, where the Scottish Human Rights Commission worked with the local committee to develop a Human Rights Policy.[54] In particular, the policy document set out how human rights would be developed and promoted within the delivery of the Games and, interestingly, included a sustainable procurement policy. The IOC has developed this approach by requiring as one of the Core Principles of the Host City Contract with Paris 2024 that the organisers:

> protect and respect human rights and ensure any violation of human rights is remedied in a manner consistent with international agreements, laws and regulations applicable in the Host Country and in a manner consistent with all internationally-recognised human rights standards and principles, including the UNGPs, applicable in the Host Country.[55]

This new focus on the protection of human rights as an integral element of hosting an edition of the Games is an important development. However, the lack of a requirement of an Olympics-specific framework for remedying human rights infringements at the Games is a major oversight. Instead, remedies are provided through the usual routes, which could take many years to resolve.

Embedding a relational approach should ensure that future HCCs create a relationship more like a marriage and less like a one-Games stand. The IOC must ensure that the host is appropriate and capable of complying with the requirements of the Olympic Charter and the Fundamental Principles of Olympism. Alternatively, it must demonstrate how lasting, positive change will be implemented as a result of hosting the Games. On the other hand, the HCC must ensure that the host is not placed under unnecessary financial, social, political, and environmental stress. A more host-specific bespoke Olympics, instead of the constant striving for the biggest and best Games ever, that provides community facilities, social housing, and does not damage the environment could be changes that ensure that a wider pool of countries are both willing and able to act as hosts. The relationality of the HCC will also ensure that athletes' rights are protected more effectively as the protections can be required as a term of hosting the Games.

Having considered recalibration on both the individual (athlete) level and the broader issue of the collective (host) level, we turn finally to the IOC itself, and the need to effect changes to its law-making capacity. It is perhaps unsurprising that as lawyers our final reflections are on this point, but as we note throughout the book and elsewhere,[56] there is a need to resolve tensions inherent in all the elements of the Olympic legal framework.

Recalibrating the IOC's law-making capacity

There is of course a tension at the heart of Olympic law. This concerns the need to protect the Olympic brand, on the one hand, and the need to promote the unique meaning of the 'brand' as defined in the Fundamental Principles of Olympism on the other. At present, the balance is in favour of facilitating the commercial exploitation of the Olympic Properties at an increasing number of IOC sanctioned events.[57] The focus on protecting the Olympic brand has, however, demonstrated the potential scope of the IOC's indirect law-making capabilities, in both the transnational and municipal spheres, by its requiring host nations to translate the *lex Olympica* into Olympic law. This indirect legislative ability could be used to recalibrate the relationship between the Olympics and its host and to ensure that Olympism is brought back to the foreground through a redrafting of the HCC's requirements and the operation of Rule 33 of the Olympic Charter. A more cooperative, or relational approach, with proper checks and balances in place, has the potential to provide an innovative means of implementing this peculiar type of transnational law.

Writing about the FIFA World Cup 2022 in Qatar, Duval noted that whilst FIFA has no direct or formal control over the employment rights of migrant workers employed to build the stadia, it maintains an indirect control through its ability to influence the conditions under which these workers operate.[58] This indirect power, exerted through the HCC, could be used in a more positive way to encourage, as opposed to forcing, these conditions to change. This would enable the IOC (and other hosts) to require, for example, that candidate cities are signatories of key instruments, or collections of instruments such as the International Bill of Rights, as a precondition of bidding to host the Games.[59] Audits and impact assessments to ensure that these rights are actually being protected as required by these instruments could form part of the candidate city pack, as are the covenants ensuring compliance with the Olympic Charter and the legal guarantees of protections for the Olympic Properties. Relationality is achieved by the requirement that the IOC must ensure that it is itself acting in accordance with the UNGPs and leading by example to ensure that the Olympic Movement as a whole is achieving these new standards that it sets for itself.[60] This could enable sports mega events to move from being a site of protest to being a positive force for change in a host country.

Future trajectories

The IOC has an extraordinary, and somewhat curious, capability to create law. The question arises, in the light of the shifts we suggest, how might this specialised form of transnational law be used in a more positive way? There are a number of possibilities. Olympic law could be enacted to reinforce the Fundamental Principles of Olympism,[61] the guiding principles or mission statement of the Olympic Movement, instead of being used almost exclusively to voraciously protect the intellectual property rights and iconography associated with the IOC and each edition of the Olympic Games.[62] By recalibrating the relationship between the transnational legal norms imposed on host nations by the IOC, it would be possible for the legal frameworks required of organising committees to be used to further both the Fundamental Principles of Olympism and improve the socio-economic rights of Olympic stakeholders. The broader socio-economic changes that are occurring alongside the growing sophistication of the critiques of hosting the Olympics, which have resulted in an increased reticence of cities to bid for the Games have created a landscape that could allow such a recalibration to be of calculable benefit to the IOC, candidate cities, and the eventual hosts. Further to this, Schwab argues that '[f]or *lex sportiva* to be legitimate as a system of law, it must, at a minimum, respect and fulfil the fundamental human rights of the people who are the subject of that law – the players.'[63] This could be seen particularly in the sphere of workers' rights, but more generally that there is a need to incorporate human rights into *lex sportiva*, *lex Olympica* and by extension, Olympic law. Only by embracing, and leading on, the inclusion of human rights into their legal frameworks will *lex sportiva* and *lex Olympica* attain the legitimacy they crave.

Our analysis adds to the wider discussions of the IOC and the Olympic Games being in an extended period of existential crisis. At its core, we have shown that there is a tension at the heart of the Olympics between what the IOC claims to stand for and what it actually protects and promotes. We have proposed a more relational approach to the easing of that tension between Olympic culture and Olympic commerce that, going forward, is in the interests of all stakeholders, and in particular of the IOC. Whilst there are many problems with the Olympics, there remain positive possibilities to renegotiate these in the future. No sooner does one edition of the Olympics finish, than another one starts, and that pregnancy is just as important as legacy. The themes and issues raised in this book, and its central thesis, can and hopefully will be tested at future editions of the Games. The cultures and values of Paris 2024, Milano Cortina 2026 and Los Angeles 2028, will be perfect petri dishes to examine these tensions, and our suggestions for tackling them.

Notes

1　Zervas, K (2012) 'Anti-Olympic Campaigns' in Lenskyj, H and Wagg, S (eds) *The Palgrave Handbook of Olympic Studies* (Palgrave, Basingstoke), ch 33.
2　See Lenskyj, H (2012) 'The Case against the Olympic Games: The Buck Stops with the IOC' in Lenskyj, H and Wagg, S (eds) *The Palgrave Handbook of Olympic Studies* (Palgrave, Basingstoke), ch 35.
3　Zervas, K. (2012) 'Anti-Olympic Campaigns' in Lenskyj, H and Wagg, S (eds) *The Palgrave Handbook of Olympic Studies* (Palgrave, Basingstoke), at 546.
4　Keys, B, (2021) 'Boycotting the Olympic Games is not enough' *Open Global Rights*, 21 July, available at: https://www.openglobalrights.org/boycotting-the-olympic-games-is-not-enough/?lang=English (last accessed 4/03/2022).
5　Parry, J (2003) 'Olympism for the Twenty-first century' Paper prepared for Centre d'Estudis Olimpics, available at: https://www.academia.edu/51610477/Olympism_for_the_21st_century (last accessed 24/04/2022).
6　We do not deal with the issue of legacy specifically in this book. A useful starting point is Tomlinson, A (2014) 'Olympic Legacies: Recurrent Rhetoric and Harsh Realities' 9(2) *Contemporary Social Science* 137–158, where Tomlinson shows that legacy was not part of Olympic rhetoric until 1988 and that it only became adopted in IOC documents in 2002. Whilst legacy is often framed as positive, it is

not always so. As Tomlinson states at 145, 'In spatial terms, Olympic events have often promised regeneration and delivered instead displacement and rebranding'. See further Boykoff, J and Fussey, P (2014) 'London's Shadow Legacies: Security and Activism at the 2012 Olympics' 9(2) *Contemporary Social Science* 253–270.

7 For a discussion of how relational contract theory and the referential theory of contracting apply to the Host City Contract, see Borowick, J (2012) 'The Olympic Host City Contract: Achieving Relational and Referential Efficiencies to Deliver the *Best Games Ever*' 12(1) *Virginia Sports and Entertainment Law Journal* 126–170.

8 Ibid, 128–9.

9 Grix, J and Lee, D (2013) 'Soft Power, Sports Mega-events and Emerging States: The Lure of the Politics of Attraction' 27(4) *Global Society* 521–536.

10 See IOC (2022) *Factsheet: Olympic host election results*, available at: https://stillmed.olympics.com/media/Documents/Olympic-Games/Future-Host/Factsheet-Olympic-host-election-results.pdf (last accessed 14/12/2022).

11 Greenfield, S and Osborn, G (2007) 'Understanding Commercial Music Contracts: The Place of Contractual Theory' 23(1) *Journal of Contact Law* 1–21, at 5.

12 See his argument on standard form contracts, and arguably his attempt to fashion a doctrine of inequality of bargaining power in *A Schroeder Music Publishing Co Ltd v Macaulay* (1974) All ER 616.

13 *Mutu and Pechstein v Switzerland*, applications nos. 40575/10 and 67474/10, available at: https://hudoc.echr.coe.int/eng#{%22fulltext%22:(%22pechstein%22),%22itemid%22:(%22001-186828%22)} (last accessed 24/02/2023).

14 Alderson, R (2015) 'Tokyo Olympic Games logo embroiled in plagiarism row' *The Guardian*, 30 July, available at: https://www.theguardian.com/artanddesign/2015/jul/30/tokyo-olympics-logo-plagiarism-row (last accessed 25/02/2022).

15 Gold, J and Gold, M (2016) 'Introduction' in Gold, J and Gold, M (2016) *Olympic Cities: City Agendas, Planning, and the World's Games, 1896 – 2020* (London, Routledge).

16 It should be noted that the cost of bids is substantial. Schnitzer and Haizinger note that the average bid budget for an edition of the Winter Olympics was $1.7bn, with the average cost of staging the event costing $2.844bn, Schnitzer, M and Haizinger, L (2019) 'Does the Olympic Agenda 2020 Have the Power to Create a New Olympic Heritage? An Analysis for the 2026 Winter Olympic Games Bid' 11(2) *Sustainability* 442–463.

17 Gauthier, R (2016) 'Olympic Game Host Selection and the Law: A Qualitative Analysis' 23(1) *Jeffrey S. Moorad Sports Law Journal* 1–67, at 4.

18 For the specific details, see https://www.olympic.org/olympic-agenda-2020 (last accessed 25/02/2022).

19 IOC (2021) *Olympic Charter*, available at: https://stillmed.olympics.com/media/Document%20Library/OlympicOrg/General/EN-Olympic-Charter.pdf (last accessed 02/03/2023).

20 Preuss, H, Scheu, A and Weitzmann, M (2021) 'Referendums at Olympic Games' in Chatziefstathiou, D, Garcia, B and Seguin, B (eds) *Routledge Handbook of the Olympic and Paralympic Games* (Routledge, Oxford), ch 17.

21 Olympic Agenda 2020, available at: https://www.olympic.org/olympic-agenda-2020 (last accessed 02/03/2023).

22 Gold, J and Gold, M (2016) 'Introduction' in Gold, J and Gold, M (2016) *Olympic Cities: City Agendas, Planning, and the World's Games, 1896 – 2020* (Routledge, London), at 12.

23 See MacAloon, J (2016) 'Agenda 2020 and the Olympic Movement' 19(6) *Sport in Society* 767–785.

24 See MacAloon, J (2016) 'Agenda 2020 and the Olympic Movement' 19(6) *Sport in Society*, at 769.

25 James, M and Osborn, G (2017–18) 'Pliant Bodies. Generic Event Laws and the Normalisation of the Exceptional' 12(1) *Australian and New Zealand Law Journal* 77–96.

26 Louw, A (2012) *Ambush Marketing and the Mega Event Monopoly* (TMC Asser Press, The Hague), at 633.

27 James, M and Osborn, G (2017–18) 'Pliant Bodies: Generic Event Laws and the Normalisation of the Exceptional' 12 (1) *Australian and New Zealand Sports Law Journal* 77–95.

28 Feinman, J (2000) 'Relational Theory in Context' 94(3) *Northwestern University Law Review* 737–748, at 738.

29 Tan provides an authoritative overview of a range of cases that embrace relational contract theory and notes that *Yam Seng v International Trade Corp Ltd* (2013) EWHC 111 (QB) is the 'poster child' of this approach: Tan, Z X (2019) 'Disrupting Doctrine? Revisiting the Doctrinal Impact of Relational Contract Theory' 39(1) *Legal Studies* 98–119.

30 Morin, J-F and Gold, E (2014) 'An Integrated Model of Legal Transplantation: The Diffusion of Intellectual Property Law in Developing Countries' 58(4) *International Studies Quarterly* 781–792.

31 See, for example, in relation to recording contracts; Greenfield, S and Osborn, G (2007) 'Understanding Commercial Music Contracts: The Place of Contractual Theory' 23(1) *Journal of Contact Law* 1–21.

32 Feinman, J (2000) 'Relational Theory in Context' 94(3) *Northwestern University Law Review*, at 741.

33 Borowick, J (2012) 'The Olympic Host City Contract: Achieving Relational and Referential Efficiencies to Deliver the Best Games Ever' 12(1) *Virginia Sports and Entertainment Law Journal* 126–170. This note was largely a thorough case study on how these theories might apply to the HCC and provided a platform for further research based on ideas emanating from the paper. The referential theory of contract is beyond the scope of this book.

34 Macneil noted in 1999 at the Northwestern Symposium that more and more support, often in unexpected areas, was given towards the relational view of contract. Under a heading of 'We are all relationists now,' he cited Posner: '(this), I hope, will be understood as a vindication of the relational contract approach' and Scott: 'All contracts are relational, complex and subjective' as examples of this. Campbell, D (2001) (ed) *The Relational Theory of Contract: Selected Works of Ian Macneil* (Sweet and Maxwell, London), at 383–384.

35 The classic is of course Macaulay, S (1963) 'Non-contractual Relations in Business: A Preliminary Study' 28(1) *American Sociology Review* 55–67.

36 Gordon, R (1985) 'Macaulay, Macneil, and the Discovery of Solidarity and Power in Contract Law' *Wisconsin Law Review* 565–580, at 569.

37 Macaulay, S (2003) 'The Real and the Paper Deal: Empirical Pictures of Relationships, Complexity and the Urge for Transparent Simple Rules' 66(1) *Modern Law Review* 44–69, at 65.

38 Frydlinger, D, Hart, O, and Vitasek, K (2019) 'A new approach to contracts' *Harvard Business Review*, September/October, available at: https://hbr.org/2019/09/a-new-approach-to-contracts (last accessed 29/03/2022). See further Frydlinger, D (2021) *Contracting in the New Economy: Using Relational Contracts to Boost Trust and Collaboration in Strategic Business Relationships* (Springer Nature, Berlin).

39 Amis, L (2017) 'Mega-sporting Events and Human Rights – A Time for More Teamwork?' 2(1) *Business and Human Rights Journal* 135–141.

40 United Nations, Office of the Commissioner for Human Rights (2011), *Guiding Principles on Business and Human Rights*, available at: https://www.ohchr.org/sites/default/files/documents/publications/guidingprinciplesbusinesshr_en.pdf (last accessed 1/03/2023).

41 Ishida, W and Wada, H (2017) 'The Implementation of the UN Guiding Principles into Daily Business Operations and the 2020 Tokyo Olympic and Paralympic Games' *Business and Human Rights Journal* 143–148.

42 Arup (2017) *Cities Alive. Rethinking legacy for hoist cities*, available at: https://www.arup.com/perspectives/publications/research/section/cities-alive-rethinking-legacy-for-host-cities (last accessed 25/04/2022).

43 Murray, C (2017) 'Rethinking legacy for host cities' *Sportcal* available at: https://www.sportcal.com/Insight/features/113109 (last accessed 25/04/2022).

44 Schnitzer, M and Haizinger, L. (2019) 'Does the Olympic Agenda 2020 Have the Power to Create a New Olympic Heritage? An Analysis for the 2026 Winter Olympic Games Bid' 11(2) *Sustainability* 442–463.

45 World Players Association (2017) *Universal Declaration of Players' Rights*, available at: https://uniglobalunion.org/wp-content/uploads/official_udpr.pdf (last accessed 01/03/2023).

46 World Players Association (2021) *World Player Rights Policy*, available at: https://uniglobalunion.org/report/world-player-rights-policy/ (last accessed 01/03/2023).

47 Flyvbjerg, B, Stewart, A and Budzier, A (2016) *The Oxford Olympics Study 2016: Cost and Cost Overrun at the Games*, Saïd Business School Working Paper 2016-20, available at: https://wayback.archive-it.org/org-467/20200808180119/http://eureka.sbs.ox.ac.uk/6195/1/2016-20.pdf (last accessed 03/05/2022).

48 Müller, M, Wolfe, S D, Gaffney, C et al. (2021) 'An Evaluation of the Sustainability of the Olympic Games' 4 *Nature Sustainability* 340–348.

49 BBC World Service (2012) 'Olympic relocations: Beijing, London 2012 and Rio' *BBC Online*, 27 January, available at: https://www.bbc.co.uk/news/world-16703402 (last accessed 02/03/2023).

50 Gold, J and Gold, M (2016) 'Introduction' in Gold, J and Gold, M (2016) *Olympic Cities: City Agendas, Planning, and the World's Games, 1896–2020* (Routledge, London), at 3.

51 Noted in MacAloon, J (2016) 'Agenda 2020 and the Olympic Movement' 19(6) *Sport in Society* 767–785.

52 Gold, J and Gold, M (2016) 'Introduction' in Gold, J and Gold, M (2016) *Olympic Cities: City Agendas, Planning, and the World's Games, 1896 – 2020* (Routledge, London), at 11.

53 Gauthier, R (2016) 'Olympic Game Host Selection and the Law: A Qualitative Analysis' 23(1) *Jeffrey S. Moorad Sports Law Journal* 1–67.

54 Glasgow 2014 (2014), *Approach to Human Rights*, available at: http://www.glasgow2014.com/sites/default/files/documents/Glasgow%202014%20-%20approach%20to%20human%20rights%20-%20December%202013.pdf (last accessed 02/03/2023).

55 Article 13(2)(b) Host City Contract Principles, available at: http://stillmed.olympic.org/media/Document%20Library/OlympicOrg/Documents/Host-City-Elections/XXXIII-Olympiad-2024/Host-City-Contract-2024-Principles.pdf (last accessed 6/03/2022).

56 James M and Osborn G (2011) 'London 2012 and the Impact of the UK's Olympic and Paralympic Legislation: Protecting Commerce or Preserving Culture? 74(3) *Modern Law Review* 410–429.

57 Owen, D (2022) 'The devil in the detail of IOC-driven qualifying event reforms' *Inside the Games*, 8 November, available at: https://www.insidethegames.biz/articles/1130171/david-blog-reforms#.Y2uB2_jjvZM.twitter (last accessed 17/02/2023).

58 Duval, A (2021) 'How Qatar's Migrant Workers Became FIFA's Problem: A Transnational Struggle for Responsibility' 12(4) *Transnational Legal Theory* 473–500.

59 González, C (2022) 'The effective application of international human rights law standards to the sporting domain: Should UN monitoring bodies take central stage?' 22(2) *International Sports Law Journal* 152–164.

60 Corrarino, M (2014) '"Law Exclusion Zones": Mega-Events as Sites of Procedural and Substantive Human Rights Violations' *XVII Yale Human Rights and Development Law Journal* 180–204.

61 Principles 1–7 of the Preamble to the Olympic Charter.

62 The Olympic Properties are defined in Rules 7–14 Olympic Charter. Further information on the meaning of the Properties can be found in: The Olympic Museum (2007) *The Olympic Symbols*, 2nd edn (Lausanne: The Olympic Museum), available at: https://stillmed.olympic.org/Documents/Reports/EN/en_report_1303.pdf (last accessed 10/8/2016).

63 Schwab, B (2017) '"When We Know Better, We Do Better" Embedding the Human Rights of Players as a Prerequisite to the Legitimacy of *Lex Sportiva* and Sport's Justice System.' 32(1) *Maryland Journal of International Law* 4-67, at 28.

Index

Note: Page numbers with "n" refer notes in the text.

For Product Safety Concerns and Information please contact our EU
representative GPSR@taylorandfrancis.com
Taylor & Francis Verlag GmbH, Kaufingerstraße 24, 80331 München, Germany